GOD, EVIL, AND INNOCENT SUFFERING

God, Evil, and Innocent Suffering

A THEOLOGICAL REFLECTION

John E. Thiel

A Herder and Herder Book
The Crossroad Publishing Company
New York

The Crossroad Publishing Company
481 Eighth Avenue, New York, NY 10001

Library of Congress Cataloging-in-Publication Data

Thiel, John E.
    God, evil, and innocent suffering : a theological reflection / John E.
    Thiel.
        p.   cm.
    "A Herder and Herder book."
    Includes bibliographical references and index.
    ISBN 0-8245-1928-0 (alk. paper)
    1. Suffering—Religious aspects—Christianity. I. Title.
BT732.7 .T54 2002
231'.8—dc21
                                2002001710

1   2   3   4   5   6   7   8   9   10   06   05   04   03   02

To the Faculty of Fairfield University

With Appreciation

~. ~

Contents

Preface

THIS BOOK EXPLORES God's relation to evil, certainly one of the perennial issues in Western thought. There is a long tradition of philosophical reflection on this topic that scrutinizes God's relation to evil by appeal to reason alone. Since the eighteenth century, this philosophical approach has taken shape in the project of theodicy, the rational defense of God before the evil of nature, humanity, and history. This study will not pursue a philosophical course through this topic, but instead will reflect on God's relation to evil theologically. Faith will guide reasoning here, and scripture and tradition, understood as divine revelation, will supply the evidence for faith-oriented reflection. The reader should not expect these reflections to lead to a familiar destination. As the history of Christian theology shows, a great variety of orthodox positions may issue from novel interpretations of scripture, tradition, and truthful experience.

The proposal that I develop focuses especially on the evil of innocent suffering. Classical Christian doctrine holds that innocent suffering does not really exist before God. My proposal begins with the assumption that it does, and considers the consequences of this assumption for the broader network of Christian belief. Even though this book deals with central Christian beliefs such as sin, grace, ethics, and the person of Christ, finally it is a book about God. Its primary thesis—that God is not the cause of death in any way—will ring strangely in traditional ears. I hope that the way I argue for this position will show itself to be compatible with traditional sensibilities.

I began to think about these issues through an undergraduate course I teach regularly on the topic of evil. I have intended to write this book for use in the undergraduate classroom and for lay readers of all ages whom I hope will find some meaning and comfort in the understanding of God presented here. I hope too that there is enough in these pages to interest fellow theologians and philosophers of religion (as critical as I am of their work!) who trouble in thought and language about God.

I completed this book in the shadow of the terrible events of September 11. The tremendous loss of life on that day highlighted the problem of innocent suffering before God in an unprecedented way for many people throughout the world. And yet, without any intent to diminish that tragedy, I want to point out that the problem of innocent suffering before God appears every day in the lives of untold millions whose suffering is not catalogued as a historical event and, in many cases, is barely even noticed. The events of September 11 surely have caused believers to reflect on the theological and pastoral implications of innocent suffering. But those reflections will be far more meaningful if they proceed from a fuller awareness of the depth of the problem in any moment and throughout history.

All biblical citations are from the New Revised Standard Version.

I have many people to acknowledge and thank as this book appears. I am grateful to Fairfield University, and especially to its Academic Vice-President, Orin Grossman, for awarding me the Robert E. Wall Research Award. This honor afforded me the time of the 2001 spring semester to write the lion's share of these pages. I am also grateful to Michael Parker, Academic Editor at Crossroad/Herder, for his thoughtful contributions to the manuscript. Several old and new friends were generous with their time in reading and criticizing drafts along the way: Paul Lakeland (yet again!), Darby Ray, Elizabeth Dreyer, John Bennett, Dennis Keenan, and Bill McConville. Other friends were supportive in other ways that helped me to stay on course: Dorothea Cook Thiel, Susan Rakowitz, Al Benney, Beth Boquet, Gregory Schopen, Randy Sachs, and Cyril O'Regan.

I am happy to dedicate this book to the faculty of Fairfield University. Fairfield has been my only academic appointment, and this book appears as I celebrate my twenty-fifth anniversary here. I do get out enough, though, to appreciate by comparison what a wonderful home Fairfield has been and is. The commitment, friendship, and support of colleagues throughout the university have had much to do with that sense, and I continue to be grateful to them for making it so.

November 7, 2001
Fairfield, Connecticut

∾ 1 ∾

Does Anyone Suffer Innocently?

THE TITLE OF OUR FIRST CHAPTER may appear odd since its answer seems so obvious. Most people would say that innocent suffering not only exists but also tragically abounds. So much of the suffering we encounter in our lives and in those of others seems to be evil precisely because it involves the suffering of the innocent. We can define "evil" as the destruction of personal life and its life-promoting environments. Evil diminishes personal life, whether through physical or emotional suffering, or whether human persons or natural circumstances cause that suffering—at worst, a suffering that brings death.[1] One could argue that innocent suffering is the evil that measures all evils. To suffer innocently is to suffer unjustly. Unjust suffering is morally scandalous. It compels its victims and those who witness its effects to contemplate the powerlessness of suffering and the wantonness of evil's destructive power. Innocent suffering prompts a reaction of outrage at the plight of the sufferer, the ignorance or willfulness of the perpetrator, or the capriciousness of the circumstances from which such suffering results. Innocent suffering, whether it appears in the life of an infant or of someone elderly, evokes a cry of lament that no moral person desires to hear but which no moral person can ignore. In many respects, it is the awful power of innocent suffering that, by way of contrast, defines our notions of morality in codes of ethics, systems of law, and in our common

1

judgments about what sorts of sensitivities and responses distinguish the moral from the immoral person.

Yet much Jewish and especially Christian belief denies the fact of innocent suffering. This denial is not a cavalier rejection, as though Jewish and Christian belief eccentrically dismisses what common sense would quickly affirm. Rather, it is consistent with what these belief systems claim about God and God's relation to evil. Since Jews and Christians make claims about the sort of being God is, denying the reality of *innocent* suffering has been important to them. This denial takes different forms, especially as we compare its Jewish and Christian versions. But its function within these belief systems is always the same—to diminish or even eliminate the tension between God's love, goodness, and power, on the one hand, and the possible scandal of innocent suffering, on the other. The denial of innocent suffering allows Jews and Christians to profess their belief in God's goodness more clearly than they believe would be possible if the reality of innocent suffering were conceded.

The denial of innocent suffering, though, exacts an enormous price of intelligibility, since it requires reason to overlook the tragic unfairness of unmerited suffering, especially when unmerited suffering is great. The denial exacts an enormous emotional price. It requires those who deny it to qualify their sympathy toward suffering that cannot, in their judgment, be innocent but only guilty. Most of all, the denial of innocent suffering exacts an enormous price of the very belief it works so hard to affirm. If innocent suffering does indeed exist, then its denial entails ignoring the troubling issue of God's relationship to innocent suffering. One might go so far as to say that the denial of innocent suffering prevents the tradition from dealing theologically with God's relationship to evil at all, if all "evils" are measured by the evil of innocent suffering.

This short book explores God's relation to evil, particularly the evil of innocent suffering. My goal is not to construct a theodicy, a rational justification of God's goodness in the face of evil. Rather, I shall be concerned with a theological treatment of God's relation to evil within the assumptions of the Christian tradition, though in a way that fully acknowledges the evil of innocent suf-

hese issues, unlike a theodicy,
ripture and tradition; its ratio-
basic Christian claims of faith.
ccount of God's relation to evil
ions that render the existence
y created universe. My aim is
ibly coexist with God or show
evil that would place it within
o offer a theologically fruitful
o the evil of innocent suffer-
f the classical assumptions of
point in doing so, however, is
as antiquated or obsolete, but
h the tradition's basic beliefs.
that the question posed by
nust be answered in the affir-

The Classical Christian Explanation of Evil

After his conversion to the Christian faith in 386, Augustine of Hippo continued to reflect on a problem that had occupied him since his youth—the nature of evil and evil's relation to God's divine goodness. Augustine, however, approached the problem differently from the course he pursued as a younger man. From the age of nineteen to shortly before his conversion, Augustine had found solace in the clear, dualistic answer to the problem of evil offered by Manicheism. Manicheism held that evil is neither humanity's fault nor the fault of a true and good God who dwelled in a spiritual dimension beyond this world. Evil is the work of an inferior, evil god who created the universe as this god's own physical embodiment. Now at the age of thirty-three and as a newly baptized Christian, Augustine began to give a different answer to this question in his most sophisticated anti-Manichean tract, *On Free Choice of the Will* (387–95).

On Free Choice is a dialogue in which Augustine's friend Evodius is cast in the role of willing conversation partner amenable to Augustine's wise direction. Evodius begins the philosophical conversation by posing the question around which the entire dialogue revolves: "whether God is not the cause of evil."[2] The Christian God, of course, is the God of the Old and New Testaments, the creator of the universe, whose handiwork mirrors the infinite goodness and love of God's own divine and eternal nature. Evil is utterly foreign to God's being and God's will. According to Christian belief, then, the shortest, most direct, and only permissible answer to Evodius's question is no, God is not the cause of evil. Augustine's answer to Evodius's question, however, is neither short nor direct but worked out slowly in the sort of careful argumentation one would expect from one of the Christian tradition's most accomplished thinkers. We can begin our study by noting Augustine's first overture to Evodius's question, in a distinction he makes between two kinds of evil and their causal relation to God.

We speak of evil, Augustine observes, in two senses—as evil that one does as a voluntary act and as evil that one suffers. If one believes "that God is good," he claims, "God does not do evil." "Also," he continues,

> if we admit that God is just (and it is sacrilege to deny this), He assigns rewards to the righteous and punishments to the wicked—punishments that are indeed evil for those who suffer them. Therefore, if no one suffers punishment unjustly (this too we must believe, since we believe that the universe is governed by divine Providence), God is the cause of the second kind of evil, but not of the first.[3]

Augustine's distinction is an interesting description of the human encounter with evil. At times we are the perpetrators of evil. Our conscience calls us to task for breaking the moral law, causing harm to ourselves, to others, or to both. At times we suffer evil that others seem to have caused or that results from circumstances seemingly beyond human control. Here the bitterness of misfortune, and not the sting of conscience, wells up first and foremost in the emotions of the sufferer who meets evil as its recipient rather than as its perpetrator.

Modern readers might be inclined to read Augustine's distinction as an ancient variation on one commonly made in modern thought between "moral" and "physical" evil. Drawing on a distinction made by the eighteenth-century philosopher Immanuel Kant, contemporary thinkers often classify evil either as the product of human freedom (moral evil) or as the consequence of a non-moral realm of natural laws that can stir suffering through the elements, disease, old age, and death (physical evil). In this modern view, physical evil enters human life as suffering and anguish but does not have a moral cause since this would require the free exercise of the will, within which responsibility for evil becomes meaningful. The suffering that many moderns might ascribe to the laws of nature, Augustine attributes utterly to divine power at work in creation. And Augustine's view, representative of traditional Christian belief, regards this power as God's just distribution of rewards and punishments to the good and the wicked respectively.

Of course, it is precisely at this point that Christian belief confronts the problem of evil, a problem that arises by trying to reconcile providence with the actual ways in which evil appears in human lives. If in this life the blatantly good were rewarded for their goodness and the evil punished for their wickedness, then a consistent divine justice would greatly diminish the problem of evil. The good would still suffer innocently. But at least the punishment or retribution suffered by the wicked would witness to the suffering of the innocent and herald God's condemnation of evil. In such a scenario, the problem of evil would still consist in God's permitting evil, even the evil of innocent suffering. But the problem of evil would pale before the clarity of divine justice.

Actual human experience runs counter to this thought-experiment. The wicked often thrive and the good suffer. Moreover, innocent suffering offers scandalous testimony to the intensity of the problem of evil for believers, a testimony repeated again and again with each passing historical moment. The innocent suffering of innumerable victims—of the Holocaust, of the Cambodian genocide, of the systematic rapes unleashed as acts of war against Bosnian women and girls, of the Gulf War and its terrible aftermath of disease and starvation in Iraq, of acts of terrorism, such as those of September 11, conducted in the name of myopic ideologies, the innocent suffering of uncountable victims

—of natural disasters, of the inexorable movement of earth, wind, fire, and water, of accident, of disease and death that come upon the young before their time, of disease and death that come upon the old and which, though expected, are judged no less to be innocent suffering—all these examples, multiplied throughout history, mark out the dimensions of the problem of evil for any believer in a God of goodness, love, and mercy.

Augustine's judgment that no suffering is innocent represents the Christian tradition's classical response to this problem. All evil, and so all suffering that stems from evil, is caused by the human will, and human persons are responsible for it. This is most clearly the case with the evil that we perpetrate, to which Augustine refers as the "first kind" of evil. As its perpetrators, human persons are the causes of evil. In Augustine's account in *On Free Choice of the Will*, evil acts entail a willful turning away from the divine law toward lesser, created goods perversely elevated to the status of God. Evil, Augustine argues, lies not in the lesser goods falsely idolized nor in the God-given condition of the human will but rather in the corruption of the divinely created and good will by an aberrant choice motivated by inordinate desire or lust. Free will in this early work possesses the capacity to follow reason's natural attraction to the goodness of God's will. But free will often serves lustful desire, choosing what is not God as though it were and in the vanity of this self-centered illusion giving rise to evil. For Augustine, now the faithful son of the church, evil is not something that exists, as the Manicheans maintained, but a nothingness, a lack, a privation, and specifically a privation of free choice properly exercised to serve the divine will.[4] Any suffering that the perpetrator of such evil incurs (and Augustine would judge the privative, evil act itself to entail a reflexive suffering) is self-caused and deserved, the lot of false choice.

Finally, Augustine makes the same judgment about the "second kind" of evil, the evil that one undergoes or suffers rather than perpetrates. In the opening passage of *On Free Choice of the Will*, Augustine goes so far as to say that God is the cause of this second kind of evil. The sufferer does not cause disease, or ill fortune beyond human agency, or the frailty of old age, or the death that comes from natural causes sooner or later in life. Only God wields power capable of inflicting such suffering. And yet, though God is the cause, such suffering is not innocent. This "second kind" of evil is the just recompense for the perpetration of evil of which all are guilty. In the end, all suffering is caused by the human will, for if the human will were not itself the agency of evil, God would have no cause to inflict the "second kind" of evil. Indeed, Augustine's logic must conclude that this evil is only evil in the distorted perception of human sinfulness. In God's eyes, such "evil" is the just punishment of the wickedness that all persons commit.

Augustine's distinction between two kinds of evil in human perception, then, quickly collapses into a single kind of evil in the objective order of things.[5] In this objective order the following statements are true: God does not do evil, though God does cause just suffering; all human persons do evil and so cause evil suffering; there is no innocent suffering. These statements, and particularly the third (which follows from the first two), express an influential Christian reading of the Genesis story of the primal sin, one that can be traced as far back in the tradition as Paul's first-century letters to nascent Christian communities. In this reading, the sin of Adam and Eve, their willful rebellion against God, is relived in the life of each and every one of their descendants. Paul judges that "all have sinned" (Romans 5:12) by inescapably following the bad example of the first parents. The proof of this unyielding pervasiveness of evil action lies in the universality of death. In Paul's interpretation of Genesis, the sin of Adam and Eve brings about death as a just divine punishment (Romans 5:16). As all of their descendants followed in the footsteps of the parents, "so death spread to all because all have sinned . . ." (Romans 5:12).

Although Paul's understanding of a captivating evil unleashed in history might be prematurely identified as a doctrine of original sin, it is important not to conflate Paul's strong view of sin and this later Christian belief. Paul does not say that the human race is born into sin as a consequence of the first parents' primal sin, as the doctrine of original sin holds. He simply says that all commit sin by their actions in life and that the inescapability of evil acts is proved by the fact that everyone dies. Indeed, in his later writings against the Pelagians (412–430 C.E.), Augustine intensified Paul's strong view of sin to the point of claiming that evil's inescapability was marked by birth as well as by death. *On Free Choice of the Will* has relatively little to say about the inescapability of sin. In fact, Augustine is so ardent to attribute evil to the power of a free choice that his opponent Pelagius decades later could cite this early work as a formidable argument against the doctrine of original sin that Augustine later advocated and bequeathed the tradition. Yet *On Free Choice of the Will* makes the consistent Christian claim that there is no innocent suffering. All human beings are guilty perpetrators, and so the evil suffered by them in any way is God's just punishment for their evil actions.

Advantages to Denying Innocent Suffering

The denial of innocent suffering has certain advantages for Christian belief that explain its appeal through the ages. In her fascinating study *Adam, Eve, and the Serpent*, Elaine Pagels expresses amazement that Augustine's doctrine of original sin, the tradition's most articulate denial of innocent suffering, has received such broad support among Christian believers since the fifth century. "Why," she asks, "did Catholic Christianity adopt Augustine's paradoxical—some would say preposterous—views" that no one suffers innocently since all are born into sin for which they are guilty, even if not personally responsible?[6] Her answer to this question looks to human need in order to explain the constancy of this Christian belief. People, she observes, "often would rather feel guilty than helpless."[7] The doctrine of original sin satisfies this emotional need. As one faces victimizing suffering, especially suffering that issues from no human will, there is a strange emotional comfort in thinking that this suffering, and finally death itself in any form, is part of an eventful drama in which the human person plays a role. As a child of Adam and Eve, the traditional belief claims, every person is guilty and so deserving of suffering and death. Evil issues from the moral sphere of the human will, which the divine will enters in order to exact just punishment. This account has flourished for so long in Christian belief, Pagels concludes, because the alternative explanation lacks such righteous, volitional symmetry. If human beings do not enact their own suffering, however indirectly through distant, primeval parents, then they are left to meet evil in life as helpless victims for whom there is no meaningful response to the question Why? In Pagels's account, innocent suffering exacts a psychological price that most Christians have been unwilling to pay, opting instead for the guilt of original sin and the concomitant justice of divine punishment.

Pagels offers a psychological perspective on the Christian denial of innocent suffering. Her explanation takes its point of departure from the human need to find comfort in suffering, particularly in the way suffering manifests human responsibility, however failed, and divine power, albeit in the form of punishment. I find Pagels's explanation to be very insightful in identifying the advantage in a Christian denial of innocent suffering. There is a greater advantage, however, in a fundamentally theological explanation, one that takes its point of departure from the nature of God.

Christians believe with their Jewish ancestors in faith that God is a person and so possesses a character. The character of God, the sort of person God is, can be described through certain qualities gleaned from judgments about how God has acted. God, for example, is creative, and extraordinarily so, because God has brought the universe into existence from nothing. God is good, and extraordinarily so, because God continues to preserve the universe and ensure the welfare of God's creatures. God is merciful, and extraordinarily so, because in the face of ongoing human sinfulness, God ever forgives. And God is loving, and extraordinarily so, because God unreservedly communicates the gift of God's eternal self to creation, even to the point of becoming human for the sake of the world's salvation (John 3:16). One might be tempted to think that these divine character traits are simply a matter of dogmatic belief—that they are ascribed to God because the religious tradition in which they are affirmed teaches authoritatively that God is like this and believers are obliged by virtue of their allegiance to the tradition to regard it as so. The tradition does claim and teach with authority that God's character is of a certain sort, but it does so on the basis of the real religious experience of believers throughout the ages who have encountered in their lives, and who continue to encounter, a God who does indeed act creatively, benevolently, mercifully, and lovingly.

Indeed, the consistency in this plethora of actual, personal encounters with God has led believers to assert that God does not merely possess character traits such as those noted above, but that these character traits *are* the divine being itself. The character-forming actions of human persons are distinguishable from their being. Different human persons who otherwise share common human traits may yet develop very different characters by their actions. A human person's character, enacted along certain lines in the course of time, may yet change as choices influence character for good or ill. God's character traits, Christians believe, are so steadfast (in traditional language, eternal) and so superlatively unique (in traditional language, simple) that they are identical with the divine being. Moreover, this identity of character and being in God defines the reality of these traits in the world God has created. God's personal being is creativity itself, goodness itself, mercy itself, and love itself. God's actions necessarily and unfailingly promulgate these traits, for these are all that God is or could ever be.

The scandalous encounter between God and evil results not only from the viciousness and extent of evil but also from the Christian belief that God is this particular sort of person, that God possesses a benevolent and loving character that believers really come to know through their own experience, and that this character exercises its power over the created world in which evil yet seems to hold sway. This clash between God and evil in the life of faith is especially pointed in the face of what might be judged to be innocent suffering. God's relation to any evil causes turmoil in the life of faith. How could God permit the realization of the evil intention of the child abuser? This is a troubling question for faith, even when it is posed theoretically and in relation to the power wielded in an evil act. But the anguish to faith is increased exponentially if we see before our eyes the actual effects of this evil intention on the victimized sufferer. The broken bones and blackened eye of a five-year-old boy and the cigarette burns on the body of a three-year-old girl plead to faith for a justification in which the God who is goodness itself can still possess integrity. Why God made a world in which sin and death were ever possible at all can be a troubling question for faith, even when it is posed abstractly as a speculative thought-experiment. But again, the anguish to faith is increased exponentially as one ponders the death of a young person, full of talent and promise, to an unyielding cancer. The body in death that no longer laughs, achieves, hopes, or enjoys the company of family and friends cries to faith for a justification in which the God who is love itself can still have a place.

Innocent suffering, in other words, presents the greatest threat to faith in God, since this suffering particularly forces believers to face the possibility of God's complicity in evil. When suffering comes to the innocent through the evil actions of others, divine complicity is diminished somewhat by the fact that the evil act is not directly willed by God. Nevertheless, the scandal of innocent suffering, even in this case, leads believers to ask why God did not intervene to prevent this evil. How, one asks, could God's providence allow such innocent suffering to occur? This indirect complicity becomes direct, and especially problematic, when innocent suffering is *not* the result of human actions. God's will alone seems capable of causing the suffering that occurs through natural disasters, disease, and death. Those who suffer from these causes seem strikingly innocent of the pain, anguish, and fate that befall them, and God's apparent complicity in such evil can call divine justice into question. Most often, when God is named as the evil perpetrator, God disappears as a reality unworthy of belief. The God of the tradition, whose very being is goodness, mercy, and love, simply cannot be reconciled with the agent of innocent suffering. And unless one follows the Manichean, and for moderns utterly mythological, road of positing two gods—one good, the other evil—naming God as evil results in the loss of faith.

There are many reasons that atheists might give for their

denial of God. The most common of them all is the scandalous juxtaposition of innocent suffering and the God of the tradition. The theological advantage of the doctrine of original sin lies in its denial of innocent suffering as a way of affirming the innocence of God. As a child of Adam and Eve, the doctrine holds, no human person is innocent, for all share in their sin through birth and so are inescapably guilty. There is a sense, then, in which the denial of innocent suffering traditionally has made belief in the Christian God possible. Along with Pagels's psychological advantage to the Christian denial of innocent suffering, we must take note of this even greater theological advantage which allows the character of God to stand amidst the most disturbing, and utterly common, suffering encountered in history. Simply put, the denial of innocent suffering lets the Christian God be the Christian God.

Evidence to the Contrary

While the denial of innocent suffering offers advantages to the believer's faith in God, it also shakes that faith's credibility when it meets actual, concrete instances of victimizing suffering. The very presence of the suffering of victims pleads its case before the tribunal of human experience, demanding that the injustice of such suffering at the very least be acknowledged and even more be redressed. The simple sense that the victim could not in any way deserve the suffering that befalls him or her stirs this sense of injustice. The victimized sufferer may be guilty of perpetrating evil and so of causing suffering to others. But the suffering now endured is judged to be out of all proportion to whatever suffering the victim may have caused, and so much so that the victimizing suffering itself cannot be placed on the same scales of justice as the victim's guilt. This inconsistency in effects between those someone evilly causes and those someone now evilly endures prompts the judgment that a person who is not perfect but yet good in character, intention, and action suffers innocently. Suffering in such a situation becomes outrageous, a matter of abuse, a scandal that even admittedly sinful sensibilities cannot abide.

Two examples may help to make the point: the suffering of Holocaust victims and the suffering of children.

Between the years 1938 and 1945, the Nazi regime directed much of its violent energy toward the destruction of the Jewish people. First through execution squads in Eastern Europe and western Russia, and then through the efficiency of the concentration camps, the Nazi regime systematically exterminated millions of Jewish men, women, and children. For many, the Holocaust offers the clearest proof of innocent suffering that history has ever produced *en masse*. Only two objections could present a different account of its grisly evidence. First, there is the long-running, hateful explanation that explains Jewish persecution and finally the Holocaust as retribution for first-century Jewish complicity in the death of Christ, itself an anti-Semitic, evil explanation that we may dismiss. Second, Jewish belief itself attributes suffering to God's righteous retribution for sin. Applied to the Holocaust, this belief would account for the death camps by looking to the sinful deeds of the Jewish people. Since this second denial of innocent suffering issues from the tradition of the victims, it merits our further attention.

If we begin with Jewish assumptions, then one possible way of explaining the suffering of Holocaust victims is by regarding it as the consequence of their faithlessness to God's covenant with the people of Israel. As shocking as this judgment may seem, especially in light of the Jewish people's abiding religious commitment throughout a long history of persecution, it is a viable one in the context of Jewish belief. According to this belief, God will continue to protect the Jewish people, providing them with land, peace, and happiness, if they practice the Law that God revealed to Moses on Mount Sinai. Their failure to keep the terms of this covenant absolves God from the promise to protect them and even invites God's punishment. Within Jewish assumptions, then, one possible explanation of the suffering of Holocaust victims is that they were guilty, individually or collectively, of violating their responsibility to the covenant, and so did not suffer innocently.

The Holocaust survivor and Nobel laureate Elie Wiesel has testified to the serious plausibility of this explanation within Jewish assumptions. While a young prisoner at Auschwitz, Wiesel witnessed what he calls a "trial of God."[8] Lasting several evenings, the trial called God to task for the horrendous tribulations of European Jewry. One rabbi served as prosecutor, arguing for God's guilt in the face of the suffering and death of the camps; another rabbi served as defender, arguing for God's innocence. It was, Wiesel remembers, a solemn proceeding. The prosecutor and the defender each called witnesses, who measured the enormity of the Holocaust against the canons of divine and human justice. When the arguments came to an end, a third rabbi serving as judge pronounced the verdict of the tribunal hearing the case, a verdict that found God guilty before the horror of genocide. And yet, in an act of fidelity unimaginable had it not taken place, the same judge called for those present to pray faithfully to the guilty God.

The verdict of God's guilt in this solemn trial is, at the same time, an admission that the victims of the Holocaust suffered innocently. We must not forget, though, that this verdict was rendered in the face of opposing arguments that affirmed God's innocence, an innocence that could only be maintained by placing responsibility on the perpetrators or on the victims as guilty violators of the divine law. Later in life, Wiesel wrote a play entitled *The Trial of God* in which he sets the hearing he witnessed at Auschwitz in seventeenth-century Shamgorod, a Polish village in the midst of a pogrom. The defender of God in that play voices the traditional Jewish denial of innocent suffering in the following words:

> What do you know of God that enables you to denounce Him? ... Think of our ancestors, who, throughout centuries, mourned over the massacre of their beloved ones and the ruin of their homes—and yet they repeated again and again that God's ways are just. Are we worthier than they were? Wiser? Purer? ... After the destruction of the Temple of Jerusalem, our forefathers wept and proclaimed *umipnei khataenou*—it's all because of our sins. Their descendants said the same thing during the Crusades. And the Holy Wars. The same thing during the pogroms. And now you want to say something else?[9]

God's defender regards the claim of innocent suffering as a capricious excuse for the guilt of the Jewish people. Only Jewish failure to keep the covenant, he insists, can explain both the history of Jewish persecution and the belief that God is ever just. Wiesel chillingly casts Satan himself in the role of God's trial defender and by doing so expresses his judgment on the cogency of the defense. Satan only offers lies that promote violence, and such a lie, Wiesel suggests, is the covenantal version of the denial of innocent suffering. Wiesel speaks for post-Holocaust generations in his vehement protest against laying the blame of Jewish persecution at the feet of its victims. At the same time, this protest announces the dramatic truth of innocent suffering in the experience of the Jewish people throughout the ages, and particularly in the Holocaust.

This judgment—that innocent suffering is scandalously unjust—can be made in faith, albeit a faith ready to challenge long-standing religious explanations of the guilt of victims. But faith is not the only source of challenge to the traditional explanation. Reason too may read the scales of justice apart from faith and arrive at the same conclusion on its own terms.

From the perspective of faith, Jewish Holocaust victims, like all the Jewish people, are a chosen people, called by God to be a "light unto the nations." God's election calls the Jewish people to a moral fidelity confirmed by their unique covenant. And yet, whatever moral standard Jewish belief sets for itself, on any reasonable analysis of the evidence there is no moral difference between the victims as a group and any other group of human beings. Some of the victims were superlatively good people whose words and deeds brought only love, hope, and happiness to the lives of relatives, friends, acquaintances, and strangers alike. Some were shunned by other persons for their consistently selfish, hurtful, and even evil actions. Most were like most other human beings, ever struggling to affirm their basic goodness amidst a history of personal failures. This moral ordinariness is what reason weighs into the balance of the suffering that Holocaust victims endured. Weighing the evidence, reason looks to the moral ordinariness of the victims as a group; takes stock of the historical, political, and social events that unleashed a violent, irrational hatred, centuries old, into a bureaucratized program of death; and concludes that those who suffered did so, even in their moral ordinariness, through no fault of their own. Granted, all do not share in this common reasoning, since some still hold the prejudices of those who built the camps, loaded the cattle cars, made the selections, and reduced life to death. Yet for women and men of good will—undoubtedly the vast majority of the human race—the facts of the Holocaust provide powerful evidence of the reality of innocent suffering and make the ascription of some guilt to the victims a violation of the most elementary, reasonable sense of justice.

The extraordinary suffering of children provides clearer and more compelling evidence of innocent suffering. My previous example suggests that it is the powerlessness of victims in the face of evil that contributes to the syndrome of innocent suffering. Along with the helplessness of victims, the syndrome includes the judgment that the evil suffered is out of all proportion to the moral culpability of the sufferer. Reason judges the mass of Holocaust victims to be innocent not because each and every one lacked moral culpability but because the suffering endured by Holocaust victims was utterly disproportionate to their moral ordinariness as a group. The extraordinary suffering of children offers a clearer and more compelling example of innocent suffering not only because children are powerless before evil, as they are before life in general, but also because they lack moral culpability of any sort.[10] As a group, their sufferings cannot be weighed against even a small measure of guilt. An absence of moral failings on their part does not offer the ingredient of vice, which, when mixed with virtue, produces the collective character of moral ordinariness. If we found the sufferings of Holocaust victims to be innocent even while acknowledging their moral ordinariness as a group, then the extraordinary suffering of children provides an even stronger and more dramatic example.

The suffering of children so rages against moral sensibilities that its injustice stands out in relief, even against the background of egregious suffering. In Wiesel's play *The Trial of God*, the prosecution's case against God is pressed by an innkeeper named Berish, who is one of the few Jewish survivors of a recent pogrom in the village of Shamgorod, a massacre that took his beloved wife and two sons. Berish's servant Maria describes him to those

assembled for the trial as a man who before his loss "was generous and warm toward everybody. . . ."[11] Now he seethes with anger
toward God for God's idleness before the onslaught. Berish's
anger is most palpable in the presence of his one surviving family member, his daughter Hanna, who, though no more than a
child, was tortured and raped repeatedly for hours as the perpetrators forced her father, overwhelmed by his captors, to watch.
Throughout the play, Hanna stands in Wiesel's script as testimony
to the particular abomination of innocent suffering, as a living
question to the supposedly providential God who watched
Hanna's torture just as her father Berish did.

The character of Hanna plays much the same role in Wiesel's
text that the "girl in the red dress" plays in Steven Spielberg's film
Schindler's List. In one extended and horrifying scene, Spielberg's
masterpiece re-creates the destruction of the Cracow ghetto.
Though photographed in black-and-white, the film offers a single
instance of color as the dress of one small girl amidst all the men,
women, and children being forcibly rounded up to be executed
turns to red before the audience's eyes. This small piece of color
personalizes and intensifies the viewer's horror in the face of evil
by focusing on the person of an innocent four-year-old. That horror is confirmed later in the film as the Nazi S.S. burn the bodies
of those killed immediately in the purge and the viewer's eyes
again meet the red dress that clothes the now limp body of the
child in a wheelbarrow on its way to the flames. In the face of such
examples, and others like them, the denial of innocent suffering
especially becomes an assault on the sense of justice that all but
the thoroughly evil possess and seek to act out in their lives.

One good indication of a sound judgment is that arguments
against it quickly show themselves to be absurd. We can find good
evidence of this in our example of the Holocaust as an instance
of innocent suffering. No doubt many Jews throughout history
have found tremendous difficulties with the claim that their suffering is due to their faithlessness to the Law. This explanation,
though, has remained viable throughout the centuries of Dias-
pora. As the culmination of that terrible history of persecution,
the focused horror of the Holocaust has made that explanation
absurd, at the very least as an account of Holocaust suffering and

for many other instances of suffering to which a false sense of guilt might otherwise be attributed. Perhaps this is why Wiesel seems to treat covenantal blame in his play not as a belief as much as an argument that must make its case before the tribunal of victims. In Wiesel's judgment, the blatant innocence of the victims reveals the argument's absurdity.

We find the same argumentive absurdity as we turn back to the Christian doctrine of Adam's sin. Again, Augustine can serve as an example. Toward the end of *On Free Choice of the Will*, Augustine refutes those who find fault with God's justice in the face of seemingly innocent human suffering. He recognizes that the suffering of children especially intensifies this sense of injustice and so feels obliged to tackle this most difficult of problems head-on. He writes:

> Some raise a greater and, as it were, more merciful objection, concerning the bodily suffering with which young children are afflicted. Because of their age, they say, children have committed no sins (assuming that their souls have not committed sin before animating their bodies). Hence they ask: "What evil have they done that they should suffer so?"[12]

Early in his career, Augustine was unwilling to deny the innocence of children. He believed, though, that children would eventually lose their innocence in adulthood, an inevitable moral fact that undercuts any charge of God's injustice in the suffering of children. "[W]hat reason is there to believe," he asks rhetorically, "that anyone should be rewarded for innocence before he could do harm?"[13] Within the context of an entire, and inevitably sinful, life, the innocence of childhood seems not to possess sufficient integrity in the face of which suffering would appear scandalous or threaten God's goodness. Later in his career, Augustine denies the innocence of children by understanding the heritage of Adam's fault as a state of original sin into which all persons were born and within which they were guilty. Here, Augustine's begrudging acknowledgment of the innocence of children means that he must supply a reason that would place such suffering within God's providence and justice. Again, Augustine offers his argument in the form of a rhetorical question:

> Since God works some good by correcting adults tortured by the sickness and death of children who are dear to them, why should this suffering not occur? When the sufferings of children are over, it will be as if they had never occurred for those who suffered. Either the adults on whose account the sufferings occurred will become better, if they are reformed by temporal troubles and choose to live rightly, or else, if because of the hardships of this life they are unwilling to turn their desire toward eternal life, they will have no excuse when they are punished in the judgment to come.[14]

Since the suffering of children cannot be considered just, Augustine's only recourse is to make children pawns in a broader game of cosmic justice. Their suffering cannot be justified in light of their own innocence, but it serves the greater purpose of disciplining their guilty parents in order to bend their wills toward the reform of their lives.

This, though, is an absurd explanation on several counts. First, it diminishes the integrity of the child's life and the sufferings that befall it. In order to avoid the scandal of innocent suffering, Augustine argues that the child's suffering is not to be reckoned with on its own terms. This is seen especially in Augustine's willingness to regard the child's suffering only as a subversion of a possible parental plea of ignorance before a future judgment of eternal condemnation. Second, it assumes that suffering children are always a moral audience for adults whose lives need moral transformation commensurate with the suffering they witness. Even if one accepts the Christian judgment that all sin in Adam and so are guilty, it does not follow that all lives are so fallen that they require the goad of the suffering child to effect a significant conversion. Suffering children can, and usually do, have good parents. Nor does Augustine's reasoning explain why, if all adults are guilty in Adam and in need of some degree of conversion, all do not have children who suffer terribly. Third, Augustine's explanation fails to consider the case of Spielberg's "girl in the red dress" or others like her, who suffered and died through a vicious act of violence or accident at the same moment as parents who thus were unable to respond morally to their child's death. Reasons like these confirm the judgment that most readers make instantly and instinctively when they first encounter Augustine's argument—that its effort to justify the suffering of the innocent is baseless and offensive.

I have provided these two examples of innocent suffering—the suffering of Holocaust victims and the suffering of children—to illustrate what most know by common sense and even a burning sense of righteousness: that innocent suffering does indeed exist and appears, moreover, with an unfortunate regularity in human experience. My choice of examples here should not give the impression that innocent suffering appears only in cases such as these. Genocide and the suffering of children do not exhaust the sphere of innocent suffering. If innocent suffering exists wherever suffering is extremely disproportionate to the guilt of the sufferer—wherever, in other words, suffering is unjust—then innocent suffering appears in the lives of all sorts of victims, not just victims of the Holocaust; in the lives of adults, not just in the lives of children. Perhaps the best example of the ordinariness and pervasiveness of innocent suffering appears in the person of Job, whose biblical story offers a minority stance on the fact of innocent suffering that counters the majority tradition's denial. A close reading of Job can help us to recover a valuable scriptural resource for our theological project.

Job as Innocent Sufferer

The biblical book of Job has been interpreted in various ways, even concerning the proper understanding of its central, suffering character. The sixteenth-century King James translation of the single New Testament reference to Job, for example, makes note of Job's "patience" (James 5:11), a mistranslation, modern scholars agree, of a Greek word better rendered as "endurance."[15] Although Job is not patient at all, and indeed indignantly willing to contend with God about the injustice of his suffering, the image of Job as the "patient sufferer" has been held consistently throughout the Christian tradition. Since the horror of the Holocaust, many Jewish writers have found Job's impatient protest against the failure of divine providence to be a powerful expression of faith's ultimate seriousness—and a legitimate one that has a long-standing heritage in the Jewish tradition.

This variety in interpretation regarding even Job's basic demeanor also has extended to issues concerning the structure of the text, though this interpretive focus seems to hold consequences especially for how the character of God is understood. Historical criticism shows the book of Job to be a compilation of literary pieces that were brought together into a single story, perhaps in the sixth century B.C.E. Commentators note that the Prologue (chaps. 1–2) and Epilogue (chap. 42) possess a certain consistency in style and circumstance. This literary unity of the Prologue and Epilogue distinguishes them from the poetical speeches that comprise the large body of the work (chaps. 3–41). The most likely explanation for this difference is that the Prologue and Epilogue were originally a folktale about a righteous sufferer, Job, that the later author of the biblical book employed as a framing story for the poetical speeches on the struggles of faith in the face of suffering.

Once this compositional difference is acknowledged, there is justification for interpreting the folktale and the speeches as two separate texts. And the respective contents of the folktale and the speeches offer plenty of motivation for doing so. After introducing Job as a man "blameless and upright, one who feared God and turned away from evil" (1:1), the Prologue recounts a scene in God's heavenly court that is horrifying to a believing reader. Among the heavenly beings who present themselves to God is Satan, not the demonic personification of evil of later Christian belief but an angel who possesses a contentious relationship with God. God begins their encounter by asking Satan if he has considered Job in the course of his wanderings in the world. God flaunts Job to Satan as the faithful servant he believes Job to be, one who could never be seduced from faithfulness to God by temptation of any sort. Seeing God's pride and judging it a weakness, Satan strikes at God's confidence by explaining Job's faithfulness as self-interest:

> Does Job fear God for nothing? Have you not put a fence around
> him and his house and all that he has, on every side? You have

blessed the work of his hands, and his possessions have
increased in the land (1:9–10).

Satan continues by proposing that God "stretch out [God's] hand
now, and touch all that [Job] has," an infliction of tragedy that
Satan predicts will move Job to curse God (1:11).

To the believing reader's horror, God agrees to these terms,
becoming through Satan the agent of destruction to Job's property and the agent of death to Job's servants and children. Shock-
ingly, Job's profession of loyalty to God in the midst of these
tragedies does not dissuade God from accepting Satan's further
challenge that Job's suffering has not been pressed far enough.
For Job's hidden treachery to be revealed, Satan insists, God must
touch "his bone and his flesh" (2:5), a proposal that this easily
tempted God accepts by inflicting Job "with loathsome sores . . .
from the sole of his foot to the crown of his head" (2:7). Before
the first round of his undeserved suffering, Job had summoned
the faith to bless God's name (1:21), a testimony that should have
quelled God's desire for another test. Job's second, and bodily,
round of suffering produces no such praise of God on Job's part
but leads instead to the book of Job's "second" text, in which Job
insists on his innocence, while not cursing God, and Job's friends
defend God, often by assuming what God feared—that Job in fact
had cursed God in his heart and that his hidden faithlessness is
the cause of his tribulations.

The cycles of speeches presented in chapters 3–41—by Job, his
friends, and finally God—assume that God's ways are not the ways
of humans. This assumption appears in Job's stinging indictment
of God's injustice before his self-confessed innocence. God, Job
holds, has not been faithful as Job has. This assumption appears
again in the friends' quick defense of God and condemnation of
Job. God, the friends assert, is not a liar as Job is. Finally and most
importantly, this assumption appears a third time in God's blus-
tery proclamation of divine transcendence as a rebuff to the
Jobian question "Why me?" God's hiddenness is always an issue
throughout these middle chapters, but nowhere more than in
God's physical appearance to Job (38:1; 42:5), a theophany that
serves precisely to bolster God's divine otherness before the

uncomfortable fact of Job's torments. In chapters 38–41, God chides Job's indictment of the divine justice by posing a series of rhetorical questions whose purpose is the assertion of God's might and majesty as the providential Lord of creation:

> Where were you [Job] when I laid the foundation of the earth? (38:4)
>
> Have you commanded the morning since your days began . . . ? (38:32)
>
> Can you lift up your voice to the clouds, so that a flood of waters may cover you? (38:34)
>
> Who provides for the raven its prey, when its young ones cry to God, and wander about for lack of food? (38:41)
>
> Is it at your command that the eagle mounts up and makes its nests on high? (39:27)

God's questions, sometimes asked in an explicitly sarcastic manner,[16] remind Job that the daunting reality of divine providence cannot be reduced to human conceptions or expectations, even conceptions and expectations of divine goodness, justice, and faithfulness. Their effect is to reduce Job to silence.

Is it any wonder that some contemporary commentators have preferred to find the real theology of the book of Job only in this mysterious God who speaks from the whirlwind, a God who seems so much more worthy of belief than the Prologue's capricious tormentor of Job and the Epilogue's equally capricious restorer? And does not the redactional history of the text encourage such an interpretive division between the Jobian folktale of the Prologue and Epilogue, on the one hand, and the elegant speeches of the mysterious God, on the other?

A good example of what James G. Williams calls the "most recent tendency in biblical scholarship . . . to 'save the text' of the book of Job by viewing the speeches of God (chaps. 38–41) as integral to the original work"[17] is found in a recent interpretation by Paul Lakeland. In Lakeland's judgment, there are three "Gods" in the book of Job. The first is the "petty tyrant of the legend, who all but destroys Job in order to prove to the avenging angel that Job's love for God is disinterested." The second God is "the God of the theology of retribution . . . present in the consciousness of

Job's friends and Job himself. . . ." The third God is the God of the theophany, who speaks to Job out of the whirlwind. This God is "at least for the author and eventually for Job . . . the real God, a figure infinitely more terrifying and believable than either of the other two."[18]

Lakeland sees the book of Job as a resource for a postmodern apologetics, an account of the Christian message that can still be intelligible to a contemporary culture in which mystery lies within, not outside of, the universe, and humanity occupies no special place in the evolutionary order of things. Such an apologetics must speak meaningfully of God and humanity within the assumptions of a secular worldview. To do so effectively, Lakeland believes, this exercise in theological outreach must place a high value on human agency and responsibility while rejecting an anthropocentrism that extends God's providence in some protectionist manner to every human life. These assumptions yield an interesting, contemporary interpretation. The God of the theophany is providential, Lakeland claims, but over the whole of creation, not its parts. Job's indictment of God misses the mark because it is an indictment of the "first" or the "second" God in Lakeland's interpretive schema, but not the "third" and "real" God of the text's author. Such a God offers no response to the Jobian question "Why me?" since the question "assumes a God who makes just the kinds of distinctions in providence that the book of Job rejects." God is the God of all creation, Lakeland maintains, and so God's providence extends over the whole of the universe, but not in such a way that providence becomes "intrusive and constant attention to the predicament of each individual." The "real" God of the theophany erases "the traditional understanding of providence."[19]

There are many reasons to appreciate Lakeland's creative interpretation of Job within the context of his theological project. Here, though, I need to raise a critical question about his decision (as Williams noted, a common one among contemporary interpreters) to distinguish different "Gods" in the text and to valorize the God of the theophany. Although the text can allow for such a reading, and historical-critical investigation into the multiple literary layers within the text can lend support to it, the fact remains that the book of Job found its way into the biblical canon as a single book.[20] Perhaps the author/redactor of the canonical book of Job intended the tensions between the various appearances of God in the text to evoke exactly the sort of judgments that Lakeland expects, so that the very point of the book of Job is to recognize the God of the theophany as the "real" God whose pronouncements offer an authentic response to human suffering. But even if that were the case (and the author's intention, if discernible, somehow could carry interpretive weight across the ages!), then one would still need to explain how *this* actual, single book came to be accepted into Judaism's, and eventually Christianity's, collection of sacred writings, since traditional Judaism and Christianity do claim that God's providence extends to individual human lives. However unrealistic the Epilogue of Job may be judged to be in its account of God's abundant restoration of Job's family and property, does it not convey the Jewish and Christian belief in a God who, finally at least, is covenantally or eschatologically faithful? Jews and Christians throughout the ages who have been able to answer this question affirmatively—certainly the vast majority—have been able to read the God of the Epilogue consistently as the God of the theophany and the Prologue.

There is no doubting, though, that the book of Job is about the tension between the providential God of the tradition and the disturbing presence of suffering in human lives. It is precisely because of this tension, I would suggest, that one must insist on a kind of strained coherence between and among the "Gods" of the Prologue, the theophany, and the Epilogue. This coherence presumes that these are not different "Gods" but, at most, different ways of encountering the one God of the tradition. In this respect, the disturbing way in which the Prologue presents the God of the tradition is particularly important for a consistent reading of the book of Job, as well as for the concerns of our chapter. This consistency is not one in which the text is read from the Epilogue backwards, the interpretive direction for reading this text that most secured its place in the sacred canon. Rather, this consistency is one set from Prologue to Epilogue.

Recent interpreters quickly dismiss the God of the Prologue, judging this God of the adapted folktale to be irreconcilable with the Jewish or the Christian God. And this is not surprising. The book's author/redactor provides the reader with an extraordinary access to this God, with a peephole, so to speak, into the heavenly court. What one sees prompts this dismissal, for what one sees is terrible. The God of the Prologue is too insecure and obtuse to recognize the emptiness of Satan's taunts, choosing instead to put Job to the test by visiting his life with loss, grief, physical suffering, and the anguish of betrayal. This does not seem to be the God in whom Jews and Christians believe. Yet the events of the Prologue—and so the Prologue's God, who causes nearly all of them to unfold—are crucial for the reader's knowing what any other onlooker to Job's suffering could never know with certainty—that his suffering is innocent.[21] Placed in the position of extraordinary knower, the reader of the Prologue is forced to dismiss not the Prologue's God but all the defenses of this God offered by Job's neighbors and all the lofty claims for the cosmic demands of providence asserted by God in the theophanous speeches. The reader who takes the Prologue seriously cannot infer from Job's eventual silence any change of mind on Job's part about what God is like, or any concession on Job's part before the divine defense, other than a judgment about the futility of dialogue. Knowing what she or he knows from the Prologue, the reader can only feel uneasy in the face of Job's restoration in the Epilogue, for Job's restoration does not obliterate his innocent suffering. The refusal to dismiss the God of the Prologue makes the book of Job, from beginning to end, an uncompromising portrayal of the problem of innocent suffering, and not at all a writing that, read selectively, offers us a more adequate view of God.

My point is not that the Prologue paints a faithful picture of the God of the tradition. It does not. But it does give an honest account of how the God of the tradition, supposedly a God of love, justice, and promise, often seems to believers in the midst of terrible tragedy. The author of Job fully acknowledges the innocence of such suffering and in doing so gives voice to a common experience in the life of faith, which the logic of the covenant and the logic of the doctrine of original sin attempt to explain away. So understood, the book of Job finds acceptance into the canon not only through the Epilogue's restorative happy ending but also

DOES ANYONE SUFFER INNOCENTLY?

through the text's consistent willingness to acknowledge the reality of innocent suffering alongside the belief that God's providence extends to the lives of individuals as well as to the whole of creation.

The World of Innocence (and Guilt)

This last point, particularly as it emerges through dialogue with Lakeland's postmodern reading of Job, prompts reflection on the context in which talk of innocence or guilt becomes meaningful. Innocence and guilt presuppose the world of persons and the relationships that ensue between and among them. As judgments on the moral condition of persons before the fact of suffering, innocence and guilt presume that persons should be morally responsible toward each other, whether they be lifelong friends or strangers whose lives happen to intersect. Innocence and guilt portray moral, ontological, and psychological states that persons occupy in this expected relationship of responsibility. Guilt is the judgment (or the condition or the feeling) that a person has failed in moral responsibility to (an)other person(s), and in that failure has caused suffering of one kind or another. One may speak of degrees of guilt that correspond to the degree of moral failure and the extent of suffering that results from failure. Innocence is the judgment (or the condition or the feeling) that a person has not failed in his or her moral responsibility to (an)other person(s), and in that moral integrity has not caused suffering. There are not degrees of innocence, though a person innocent in one respect may be guilty in another. Guilt and innocence are not mutually exclusive moral states but coexist in the lives of moral persons.

Speaking of innocence and guilt as a judgment (or condition or feeling) about the moral quality of personal relationship means that one can speak meaningfully of innocent suffering only in the world of persons in relation. The gazelle that becomes the lion's kill does not suffer innocently, nor is the lion guilty for taking the gazelle as prey. The human being who whimsically and intentionally inflicts pain on a helpless animal certainly is guilty of moral failure before the community of human persons, though the animal in pain does not suffer innocently.[22] By contrast, the human being who is physically assaulted by another in an effort to rob him of his money suffers innocently.

At first glance, these examples might suggest that only suffering inflicted by one human being on another makes for innocent suffering. In the realm of relationships between and among human persons, innocent suffering indeed appears in the pain of a person victimized, through no proportionate guilt of their own, by another person's guilty action. But it is important to remember that Jewish and Christian belief insists that the world of persons, and thus of personal relation, is not exhausted by humans. God is also a person. And as a person who stands utterly in relation to other persons, God enters into the web of relations characterized by innocence and guilt. In this sphere of personal relation that includes God, suffering not caused by any human agent—the suffering caused by natural disaster, illness, or old age—could issue, in principle, from the divine agent, who wields sufficient power to be the cause of sufferings such as these. And since God is a person, whom Jews and Christians claim is related to other persons, such suffering, though not caused by human persons, could be regarded as innocent suffering if God were its cause and its human victims were not themselves guilty of inflicting it.

The author of Job leaves no doubt that Job suffers innocently. The God of the Prologue (and, I have argued, of the entire text) is a person who fails in moral responsibility to Job and who in doing so is guilty of inflicting innocent suffering. The author of Job does not envision that human agents exclusively are the cause of Job's suffering in order then to pose the question of how a faithful God could allow such innocent suffering to occur. Rather, the God of Job is a capricious perpetrator of innocent suffering that, in a world of theistic belief, only God could inflict.

We have seen that there are at least two ways to absolve God of the guilt that the author of Job, in my reading at least, attributes to God. The first, nontraditional way is to affirm a God who differs significantly from the God of the tradition. Lakeland's understanding of the "real" God of the Jobian theophany is a good example of this approach. God is absolved of guilt in Lakeland's interpretation because God's providential, and thus moral, responsibility does not extend to individual human lives. The second, traditional way of absolving God of guilt is by affirming either the Jewish doctrine of covenantal relationship or the Christian doctrine of original sin. Each doctrine, as we have seen, regards all suffering as a consequence of human guilt. The traditional accounts assume that God stands in moral relation to human guiltiness as the innocent and just exactor of divine retribution.

These two ways of absolving God of guilt are, at the same time, effective ways of denying innocent suffering. In Lakeland's reading of Job, Job's suffering is not innocent before God since God is not providentially involved in the particulars of human lives. Lakeland, of course, rejects any view that finds Job guilty or that attributes Job's suffering to divine retribution. And Lakeland would certainly claim that Job's sufferings are innocent before the community of human persons, even though Job's suffering is not caused by guilty human actions. Since Job's suffering derives from natural contingencies far from God's personal concern, however, the issue of human innocence or guilt in relation to the God of creation simply does not arise in Lakeland's reading. Job, who here represents all human beings, does not suffer innocently before God because, Lakeland concludes, God and human beings do not have the sort of relationship in which guilt or innocence appear at all. The traditional doctrines of covenant and original sin deny innocent suffering by making all suffering the guilty consequence of human sin.

As different as they are, then, Lakeland's revisionist theology and the traditional doctrines of covenant and original sin deal with the scandal of innocent suffering before God by denying its existence. This denial derives from a powerful religious desire to protect God from guilt. It requires revisionist or traditional believers in God to eliminate innocent suffering from relationship to the God they affirm, and, by doing so, to remove from theological explanation an important dimension of human experience evinced by reason and emotional common sense. Our next chapter explores the project of theodicy as a third expression of the same desire to protect God from guilt through the theological denial of innocent suffering.

Notes

1. See *The Problem of Evil*, ed. M. M. Adams and R. M. Adams (Oxford: Oxford University Press, 1990), 1; Hans Kessler, *Gott und das Leid seiner Schöpfung: Nachdenkliches zur Theodizeefrage* (Würzburg: Echter, 2000), 9–11.

2. Augustine, *On Free Choice of the Will*, trans. A. Benjamin and L. H. Hackstaff (Indianapolis: Bobbs-Merrill, 1964), 3.

3. Ibid.

4. Ibid., 83–84.

5. Ibid., 125–26. For a study of Augustine's career-long preoccupation with evil, see G. R. Evans, *Augustine on Evil* (Cambridge: Cambridge University Press, 1982).

6. Elaine Pagels, *Adam, Eve, and the Serpent* (New York: Random House, 1988), 145.

7. Ibid., 146.

8. Wiesel speaks movingly of his recollection of this event in the BBC video series *The Long Search*. See the installment entitled "The Chosen People" (New York: Time Life Video, 1977).

9. Elie Wiesel, *The Trial of God* (New York: Schocken Books, 1979), 133–34.

10. It is worth noting that this is not a traditional Christian judgment. The later Augustine articulated what was to become the traditional Christian position on this matter when he explained the wails of the child in the reception of baptism as the resistance of original sin to the grace-giving water. See Augustine, "On Grace and Free Will," in *Saint Augustine: Anti-Pelagian Writings*, Nicene and Post-Nicene Fathers 5, trans. P. Holmes et al. (Grand Rapids: Wm. B. Eerdmans, 1971), 463.

11. Wiesel, *Trial of God*, 104.

12. Augustine, *On Free Choice of the Will*, 140.

13. Ibid.

14. Ibid., 140–41.

15. See R. A. F. MacKenzie, S.J., and Roland E. Murphy, O.Carm., "Job," in *The New Jerome Biblical Commentary*, ed. R. E. Brown, S.S., et al. (Englewood Cliffs, N.J.: Prentice Hall, 1990), 466.

16. As only one example, consider Job 38:19–21: "Where is the way

to the dwelling of light, and where is the place of darkness, that you may take it to its territory and that you may discern the paths to its home? Surely you know, for you were born then, and the number of your days is great!"

17. James G. Williams, "Job and the God of Victims," in *The Voice from the Whirlwind: Interpreting the Book of Job,* ed. L. Perdue and W. C. Gilpin (Nashville: Abingdon Press, 1992), 208.

18. Paul Lakeland, *Postmodernity: Christian Identity in a Fragmented Age* (Minneapolis: Fortress Press, 1997), 96.

19. Ibid., 97. The works of Sallie McFague are the best-known representatives of this view of divine providence. See Sallie McFague, *Models of God: Theology for an Ecological, Nuclear Age* (Philadelphia: Fortress Press, 1987); *The Body of God: An Ecological Theology* (Minneapolis: Fortress Press, 1993).

20. Robert Gordis makes the point that any theory about multiple compositional strata in the book of Job must always acknowledge that "the existence of one book of Job is a *datum*" (Robert Gordis, *The Book of Job: Commentary, New Translation, and Special Studies* [New York: Jewish Theological Seminary of America, 1978], 578).

21. In his interpretation of the text, Gustavo Gutiérrez makes the compelling point that innocent suffering in history is preponderantly the suffering of the poor. See Gustavo Gutiérrez, *On Job: God-Talk and the Suffering of the Innocent,* trans. M. J. O'Connell (Maryknoll, N.Y.: Orbis Books, 1987).

22. We may speak of the innocent suffering of animals, and some people do. I suggest, though, that such talk is either an anthropomorphic rhetoric or a way of speaking of human guilt, when human actions cause such suffering.

~ 2 ~

Meaning That Eclipses Innocence

Suffering and Divine Power

in Modern Theodicies

The previous chapter distinguished two ways of denying innocent suffering in order to protect the goodness and justice of God. The traditional way is found in the classical Jewish doctrine of the covenant and the classical Christian doctrine of original sin. These ancient teachings share a willingness to deny the innocence of suffering by maintaining the sufferer's inescapable guilt. The nontraditional way appears in revisionist interpretations of divine providence such as Paul Lakeland's reading of Job. This approach so widens the scope of providence that natural human suffering can no longer be brought into focus by God's caring eye. In this nontraditional understanding of providence, natural suffering that otherwise could fall under the divine power and stand in moral relationship to a personal God is not a matter of innocence or guilt at all, but simply a contingent occurrence, however unfortunate, on the wrong side of the probability curve. By maintaining God's undiminished providence, the traditional way denies innocent suffering absolutely. By narrowing the scope of divine providence, the nontraditional way denies innocent suffering from natural causes while allowing for innocent suffering through guilty human agency. Both explanations find a theological advantage in their different ways of denying innocent suffering.

In addition to the traditional or "premodern" way and the nontraditional or "postmodern" way, there is a third way in which innocent suffering is denied to defend God's goodness and justice. This way is modern by virtue of the confidence it places in the power of human reason, specifically in reason's ability to construct a logical defense of God's goodness and power in the face of evil. Such a reasonable defense of God has come to be known as a "theodicy," following the title of the influential book of 1710 by the German philosopher Gottfried Wilhelm Leibniz.

The classical expression of the problem of theodicy appears in Western philosophy as a dilemma posed to theistic belief by evil. In the formulation of David Hume in his *Dialogues Concerning Natural Religion* (1779),

> Is [God] willing to prevent evil, but not able? then he is impotent. Is he able, but not willing? then he is malevolent. Is he both able and willing? whence then is evil?[1]

The traditional Christian understanding presupposes that God is both all-powerful and all-good, raising logical difficulties for belief in such a God, given both the fact and the proportions of evil. If God were all-powerful, then God would be able to prevent evil from ever occurring in the created order. And if God were all-good, then God would seem to have the motivation to prevent evil. Taken together, these divine attributes make the fact and proportions of evil in the world logically difficult to fathom. Were only one of these attributes ascribed to God, the logical dilemma would unwind and with it the pointed scandal of *this* God's relation to evil. If God were all-powerful but less than all-good, then perhaps God's limited will would be less than inclined to prevent evil—an unhappy prospect for believers whose faith would expect more of God, though an able resolution to the logical dilemma. Or if God were limited in power while yet possessing an unlimitedly good will, then God would seem to have every motivation to prevent evil though perhaps insufficient power to do so. This state of affairs would not necessarily be an unhappy prospect for believers, since any number of contemporary theists have found a process conception of God—in which God's power is great but not absolute—to be religiously attractive. Although the classical theist might be troubled by the prospect of a divine power short of omnipotence, such a compromise also would be an able resolution to the logical dilemma of God's relation to evil.

The problem of evil to which theodicy responds appears in the tension of this dilemma, as the belief in a God who is all-powerful and all-good meets the fact and extent of evil. Theodicy addresses the dilemma by defending God before the evil of the world. Etymologically, the word "theodicy" means the justification of God. This justification is philosophical rather than theological. It appeals to evidence reason can marshal in defense of God, rather than to evidence drawn from the assumptions of faith. As has already been noted, theodicy as a philosophical project is a modern endeavor that first appeared in the work of thinkers at the turn of the eighteenth century and has flourished particularly in the writings of contemporary British and American philosophers of religion.

My concern in this chapter is to show how the mainline theodicies, like Lakeland's postmodern theology of providence, follow the classical doctrines of covenant and original sin in diminishing the integrity of innocent suffering before God. By positing a similarity between the ancient Jewish and Christian doctrines, on the one hand, and modern theodicies, on the other, I do not mean to suggest that there are not important differences between them. In fact, their differences are striking. The ancient doctrines are shaped from the biblical narratives that Jews and Christians believe to be the Word of God and which, as divine revelation, possess an authority that supersedes the claims of reason.[2] The modern theodicies, by contrast, typically construct their logical justifications of God's goodness without appeal to the authority of revelation. The coherence of the "better argument" in negotiating the classical dilemma of God's power and goodness before evil authorizes a theodicy to present itself as a satisfactory resolution. The ancient doctrines do not justify God in an environment of hostile criticism as theodicies do. Rather they frame the conditions of human responsibility toward God within the circle of belief. Yet, in spite of these fundamental differences, the ancient doctrines and the modern theodicies both diminish the reality of innocent suffering so that God's goodness can be uncompromisingly affirmed.

There are a multitude of theodicies that might illustrate this consistent neglect of innocent suffering in the Western theological and philosophical traditions.[3] My purpose in this chapter, however, is not to catalogue and assess the varieties of the theodicy project but to show how they generally pursue the same line with regard to innocent suffering as the doctrinal tradition. I hope to prove my point by examining two broad types of theodicy. Following a well-established precedent, I shall call the first type a "best-of-all-possible-worlds" theodicy, and, coining a new rubric, I shall call the second type a "best-of-all-possible-Gods" theodicy.

The "Best-of-All-Possible-Worlds" Theodicy

The "best-of-all-possible-worlds" theodicy defends God's goodness and power by arguing that the constitution of the world, as divinely willed, must leave room for the possibility of evil if God's goodness is truly to be manifest in the world. This theodicy typically is identified with the work of the early modern philosopher Gottfried Wilhelm Leibniz (1646–1716), and so it will serve here as a first illustration of this type. The work of two contemporary philosophers of religion—John Hick and Richard Swinburne—will also be enlisted as examples of this approach.

Gottfried Wilhelm Leibniz

In 1710, Leibniz published a book entitled *Theodicy: Essays on the Goodness of God, the Freedom of Man and the Origin of Evil,* in which he argued that God's goodness could be justified logically before the evil of the world in light of a certain understanding of how God created the world. Those who fault God for the world's evils, Leibniz acknowledges, often argue that "God did not choose the best course in creating this world" since "[w]hoever makes things in which there is evil, and which could have been made without any evil, or need not have been made at all, does not choose the best course." And whoever does not choose the best course, the argument continues, "is lacking either in power, or knowledge, or goodness."[4] The conclusion that follows from such premises is that the existence of evil subverts the power, or knowledge, or goodness of God, a logical result that presents a devastating challenge to traditional theistic belief. Leibniz's answer to this argument finds a theoretical unity in the power, knowledge, and goodness of God at the very point his opponent finds only contradiction.

The scope of divine knowledge, Leibniz insists, is infinite. Its range comprehends the actual world that God created and also the infinite number of possible worlds that might have been brought into existence had God so willed. The actual world itself stood among these possible worlds prior to its creation. God creates the world as an expression of God's infinite goodness, and to do so God's divine knowledge, not different at all from the divine wisdom, surveys the infinite field of possible worlds in order to choose the best and will it into reality. "One may say," as Leibniz does,

> that as soon as God has decreed to create something there is a struggle between all the possibles, all of them laying claim to existence, and that those which, being united, produce most reality, most perfection, most significance carry the day. It is true that this struggle can only be ideal, that is to say, it can only be a conflict of reasons in the most perfect understanding, which cannot fail to act in the most perfect way, and consequently to choose the best.[5]

Since God is the God of infinite goodness, God's infinite knowledge of the infinitely possible worlds must be put to the service of God's infinite power in an utterly good way, and this occurs as God chooses and creates the best of all possible worlds. This is not to say that God is bound by some metaphysical necessity to create the world God does. But a "moral necessity," born of God's own infinitely good being, binds God "to make things in such a manner that there can be nothing better," and any other result would conflict "with the supreme felicity of the divine nature."[6]

The dilemma posed by the problem of theodicy drives a logical wedge between God's infinite goodness and infinite power, requiring God to relinquish one of them and, as a consequence, the divine nature. But Leibniz recognizes no such differentiation. God's power and goodness are an uncompromising unity established by God's infinite knowledge, and this unity leads to the creation of the best of all possible worlds. Leibniz's speculative explanation is that:

> the divine Wisdom distributes all the possibles it had already contemplated separately, into so many universal systems which it further compares one with the other. The result of all these comparisons and deliberations is the choice of the best from among all these possible systems, which wisdom makes in order to satisfy goodness completely; and such is precisely the plan of the universe as it is.[7]

"Moreover," Leibniz insists, "all these operations of the divine understanding, although they have among them an order and a priority of nature, always take place together, no priority of time existing among them."[8] God's creative choosing of *this* world from all possible worlds issues from the unity of God's power, goodness, and knowledge. This unity cannot be broken by the taunts of a philosophical dilemma, for this unity abides in eternity beyond the sequence of both time and the logical ridicule that reasoning in time occasionally produces.

Leibniz's account of an utterly beneficent configuration of infinite possibility offers a philosophical version of the traditional doctrine of providence. God's choice of the actual universe cannot be less than infinitely good because God is not less than infinitely good, and God's power, knowledge, and goodness are completely one. God, therefore, must act with moral necessity to create the best of all possible worlds. Yet, if this is so, why does the universe exist as it does, so fraught with evil? Leibniz acknowledges that the goodness of human free choice is one of the divinely chosen possibles in this best of all possible worlds. Its choice by God entailed the rejection of a possible world in which human free will did not exist. By its misuse, human free choice provides occasion for the entry of evil into the actual world. A more compelling answer, however, lies in the *via negativa* woven into Leibniz's argument. If this is the best of all possible worlds, then there is an infinite number of possible worlds other than this one, all of which possess a greater measure of evil and a smaller measure of goodness than that encountered in the actual world. And given the enormity of the infinitely greater evil that our imagination can even begin to conjure up, the evil of the actual world seems to stand out in contrast as a welcome alternative to the possible horrors of creation under another divine choice.

In light of the negative contrast, evil actually seems to be meaningful in Leibniz's theodicy. The best-of-all-possible-worlds argument places any event in the actual world, at least theoretically, in the creative unity of God's power, goodness, and knowledge. This is not to say that God wills evil of any sort. But the force of Leibniz's argument lies in its assumption that the actual world, evil and all, was raised from sheer possibility to actuality by an utterly wise and good act of the divine will, and that all of this world, even its evil, shares in the providential meaning of that eternal intention that created the best of all possible worlds. As a consequence, Leibniz can find a kind of productivity in evil, given its proximity to God's creative intention. If one assumes, as one must in Leibniz's logic, that "a world with evil may be better than a world without evil,"[9] then evil itself actually can be seen to contribute to the "best possible" that this world assuredly is. To this end, Leibniz can follow the ancient Christian writers in referring to Adam's sin as *felix culpa,* a "happy fault" for its power to bring about the redemptive incarnation of the Son of God. And yet for Leibniz, unlike the ancient Christian writers, there is no irony in this description of evil, but only a cool logic that moves inexorably toward syllogistic conclusion. The evils of the world, he claims, are "only of such a kind as may tend towards a greater good."[10]

If evil's orientation is toward a greater good, then evil is neither a senseless privation nor the injustice of innocent suffering. Indeed, in Leibniz's optimistic account, so caustically satirized in Voltaire's *Candide*, the productive quality of evil becomes a sign of faith in the goodness of God's original plan of creation, and of hope in the redemptive fullness borne by every evil act and event. This purposiveness of evil in God's grand scheme obliterates the

integrity of innocent suffering. The meaning accorded to evil subverts the possibility of any real victimization, since the only kind
of evil to which Leibniz admits is evil "as may tend towards a
greater good."

Unlike the premodern account of evil, Leibniz's explanation
does not deny innocent suffering by imputing every evil to human
guilt. While acknowledging human responsibility for much of the
world's evil, Leibniz yet finds in both moral *and* physical evil the
capacity for a meaning that stems from the original plan of creation. In the best possible order of things, innocent suffering has
no place because evil ceases to be a scandal. Charged with the
meaning of divine providence, evil brings about no real injustice
and marks no real victim whose innocence cries for redress, for
the momentary appearance of innocent suffering quickly relin-
quishes its standing to the original timelessness of God's best-
possible creative act. From all eternity, the unity of God's
knowledge, power, and goodness has made what in another, less
satisfactory possible world might have been innocent suffering
into meaningful suffering in the actual world. Leibniz's theodicy
renders innocent suffering metaphysically incoherent, and does
so for the noble purpose of defending God's goodness from the
assaults of its rationalist detractors.

John Hick

John Hick would not like being cited as an example of the best-of-
all-possible-worlds theodicy. In his influential book *Evil and the
God of Love*, Hick makes a harsh assessment of Leibniz's argument, and even Leibniz's sensibilities as a theodicist. "Having
shown to his own satisfaction that we are living in the best possible world," Hick chides, "Leibniz was content to enjoy his own
comparatively comfortable lot, leaving it to those who were less
fortunate to make the best they could of it."[11] Hick faults Leibniz's
argument for indirectly concluding that God's power is limited.
Leibniz's assertion that this is the best of all possible worlds, he
suggests, is only a disguise for the inability of Leibniz's God to
make a world in which there is no evil or at least less evil than in
the present world. For Hick, Leibniz defends the classical

dilemma's horn of divine goodness by relinquishing the horn of divine power.[12]

Here, though, in my use, the rubric "best-of-all-possible-worlds" extends more widely than Leibniz's particular version of this kind of theodicy. A best-of-all-possible-worlds theodicy as a general type argues that God willed a world open to evil in order fully to manifest God's goodness. It is a kind of theodicy that argues from the way the world is, evil and all, to the goodness of God. Hick offers such a best-of-all-possible-worlds argument, which he calls the "vale of soul-making" theodicy.

Hick's provocative argument begins with a reading of the second-century Christian writer Irenaeus of Lyons. Irenaeus, Hick notes, interpreted the story of the creation of humanity in Genesis 1:26–27 in an interesting way. In this well-known passage, God wills humanity into existence by creating human persons, male and female, in God's own "image," according to God's "like-ness." Irenaeus does not understand these words to be synonyms, positing instead a distinction between them. The former, "image," refers to the nature of humanity as it first appears in any individual life in the world; the latter, "likeness," anticipates what a human person should become through moral striving, as the finitely perfected fulfillment of God's purpose. While Hick acknowledges that this interpretation of the creation story is exegetically dubious, he finds speculative merit in Irenaeus's reading for building a coherent theodicy.[13]

Like Irenaeus, Hick proposes a two-step conception of the creation of humanity. God willed humanity into existence in and through the creation and evolution of the physical universe, from inorganic matter to organic life to personal life. The result was an intelligent creature who had the "possibility of existing in con-scious fellowship with God." In Hick's judgment, this first stage in the creation of humanity was comparatively easy, presuming the divine omnipotence. The second stage in the creation of human-ity is quite different, for it does not rely on God's power but instead on human commitment. This second stage "cannot be perfected by divine fiat," Hick insists, "but only through the uncompelled responses and willing co-operation of human indi-viduals in their actions and reactions to the world in which God has placed them."[14] The second stage of human creation is one that unfolds in the course of an entire lifetime. Creation here cannot be "created ready-made" but is "developmental and teleological." "Man," Hick asserts,

> is in process of becoming the perfected being whom God is seeking to create. However, this is not taking place . . . by a natural and inevitable evolution, but through a hazardous adventure in individual freedom.[15]

God wills that human persons take up this moral quest through their own responsibility, initiative, and free choice of the will. Soul-making or, in more common language, character-building is the means by which human beings come to fruition as the perfected persons that God created them to be.

This divine plan for the moral evolution of individuals (and not, Hick specifically states, of the species or society[16]) not only presumes their creation with a capacity for free choice but also entails God's creation of a certain kind of world in which this free choice can be actualized toward moral development. Those who deny God's goodness in the face of the world's evil often find an irresolvable conflict between God's goodness and the world that believers claim God created. If God were truly good, the objection goes, why would God have created a world so fraught with evil and the suffering it brings? Hick's response involves a close examination of the assumption inherent in the question. Raising the issue in this way, he points out, assumes that human beings are pets and God their divine owner. The critic's question imagines the world as a cage in which the owner's pets dwell.[17] "Any respect," Hick argues, "in which the cage falls short of the veterinarian's ideal, and contains possibilities of accident or disease, is evidence [for the critic] of either limited benevolence or limited means, or both."[18]

Hick finds this analogy to be thoroughly flawed, since human beings are not divine pets but God's children, who can mature into responsible adults. The correct way to pose the question about the constitution of the world is not, "Is this the kind of world that an all-powerful and infinitely loving being would create as an environment for his human pets? or, Is the architecture of the world the most pleasant and convenient possible?" The correct question is rather, "Is this the kind of world that God might make as an environment in which moral beings may be fashioned, through their own free insights and responses, into 'children of God'?"[19] Hick's answer is yes. A world with pleasure and no pain would not allow for moral maturity. The "soul-making" of human persons requires a world in which evil dwells, not merely as the consequence of failed soul-making but as a necessary context in which authentic soul-making unfolds as it confronts the trials and tribulations of life.

Even though Hick understands himself to be a staunch critic of Leibniz, there is a fundamental similarity in their positions that justifies grouping them under the rubric of the best-of-all-possible-worlds type of theodicy. Hick may fault Leibniz for an alleged insensitivity to the suffering evil causes in the world and for diminishing God's power before the infinite possibilities of creation. Yet, like Leibniz, Hick argues that the actual world is just the sort of world one would expect a good God to have created. More specifically, it is just the sort of world that a divine parent would have made for children in need of moral growth to become what God intended them to be. Hick does not present a best-of-all-possible-worlds argument like Leibniz's that abstractly values the actual world against the backdrop of infinitely possible worlds. Rather, Hick's argument implicitly invokes a smaller range of possible worlds to stand in contrast to the actual world. This smaller range of alternative worlds, in fact, needs only number one, that is, a world in which evil and suffering did not exist. Compared to a possible world devoid of evil and suffering, the actual world is far better, for in it free choice, personal development, and increase in relationship to God all can be actualized through the human encounter with evil and suffering.

Moreover, Hick's best-of-all-possible-worlds theodicy resembles Leibniz's in its reluctance to acknowledge the integrity of innocent suffering. In Hick's account, suffering is educative. It is necessary for soul-making since its absence would not allow for the transcendence through which the self becomes more Godlike. The evil of the world, then, is always meaningful, since a world in which evil is able to flourish must have been willed into existence by God for a higher purpose. Such suffering always makes meaningless victimization a lost opportunity, and innocent suffering a failure. Innocent suffering, after all, requires that the sufferer bears no responsibility for the suffering endured. Hick certainly does not argue that all suffering is deserved, like the traditional denial of innocent suffering. But Hick's theodicy makes much of human responsibility in the face of suffering, not in the sense that humanity finally is to blame for the suffering it endures but in the sense that individuals are responsible to transform suffering from mere innocence into meaningfulness. Suffering, in Hick's account, is not something to lament—the rhetoric of innocence[20]—but something to accept as an opportunity for moral cultivation.

Hick seems to recognize that the fact of innocent suffering is not irreconcilable with the actual world his theodicy interprets. He acknowledges that what he calls "excessive," or "undeserved," or purposeless suffering remains "unjust and inexplicable," "a real mystery, impenetrable to the rationalizing human mind" that "challenges Christian faith with its utterly baffling, alien, destructive meaninglessness." Nevertheless, Hick cannot allow this acknowledgment to stand but a moment before he proposes that it be something else. "And yet at the same time," he continues,

> detached theological reflection can note that this very irrationality and this lack of ethical meaning contribute to the character of the world as a place in which true human goodness can occur and in which loving sympathy and compassionate self-sacrifice can take place. "Thus, paradoxically," as H. H. Farmer says, "the failure of theism to solve all mysteries becomes part of its case!"[21]

Innocent suffering, at Hick's hand, instantly becomes meaningful suffering.

This same tendency to undercut the viability of innocent suffering so that God's goodness in creating the world can remain intact is highlighted by the criticism that Hick offers a theodicy only for survivors. Although Hick concedes the existence of purposeless suffering, he never seems to consider its most horrible consequences. As noted above, purposeless suffering quickly becomes purposeful suffering in Hick's account. And in order to become purposeful it must be meaningful for someone who still has a character capable of building. But what of the victim who cannot learn morally from suffering, the victim who is innocently victimized to death? What of innocent suffering that is wrenchingly scandalous precisely because the sufferer can no longer raise innocence to purpose? Hick's explanation would always turn discussion back to the living witnesses of such utter victimization, witnesses capable of transforming sheer innocence into a meaning that could posit God's goodness in suffering. This avoidance of the victim, however, conveys the lengths to which a best-of-all-possible-worlds theodicy will go in order to obscure or even deny the status of innocent suffering.

Richard Swinburne

A third illustration of the denial of innocent suffering in the best-of-all-possible-worlds type of theodicy appears in the work of Richard Swinburne. In an essay entitled "The Problem of Evil," Swinburne acknowledges his indebtedness to Hick[22] and defends Hick's position against the criticisms of an imaginary opponent, the antitheodicist. He does so by representing four objections raised by the antitheodicist and refuting each in turn. It is Swinburne's response to the second objection that is of particular interest to us.

Swinburne carries Hick's banner first by meeting the antitheodicist's objection that "a creator able to do so ought to create only creatures such that necessarily they do not do evil actions." Swinburne rather easily counters in typical best-of-all-possible-worlds fashion by noting that such an imagined world by definition would leave no room for free will, and that the greater good of free will necessarily entails the possibility of its misuse.[23] Even if the antitheodicist could grant a consistency between God's goodness and a free choice that may be misused, he or she would still raise the issue of innocent suffering. A creator "able to do so," the opponent presses,

> ought always to ensure that any creature whom he creates does not cause passive evils, or at any rate passive evils which hurt creatures other than himself. For could not God have made a world where there are humanly free creatures, men with the power to do evil actions, but where those actions do not have

evil consequences, or at any rate evil consequences which affect
others . . . ?[24]

The objector's concern is justice, and more particularly the scandal of innocent suffering as a grave injustice. If the presence of
free will, even with the evil it enacts, is indeed a greater good than
the absence of free will, then would it not be an even greater good
if the evil caused by free choice were suffered only by the evil perpetrator and not by innocent victims of passive evil?

At first, Swinburne rehearses typically Hickean responses to
this criticism. "A world in which no one except the agent was
affected by his evil actions," he claims, "might be a world in which
men had freedom but it would not be a world in which men had
responsibility."[25] Following Hick, Swinburne argues that passive
evil suffered by victims provides opportunity for persons to rise
to the moral occasion. By their enacted responsibility, moral
agents make innocent suffering productive, a resource for educa-
tion in virtue and the only means by which character can be built.
And like Hick, Swinburne invokes the parent–child analogy to
exemplify God's relationship to humanity. The parent raising
children does not interfere too quickly in their quarrels, "even at
the price, sometimes, of younger children getting hurt physically." The advantage in such allowance, on any parent's part, is
that children are trained "for responsibility in later life" and that
"responsibility here and now is a good thing in itself."[26]

To this point, there is little difference between Hick and Swinburne. Both offer a best-of-all-possible-worlds theodicy that
makes passive evil meaningful, thereby removing the scandalous
sting of innocent suffering. A difference between the two does
emerge in the lengths to which Swinburne is willing to go in eras-
ing the integrity of innocent suffering.

Even if the antitheodicist would be willing to concede the
meaningfulness of passive evil, the quantity and intensity of evil
in the world are still an issue that he or she would want to press
further. Innocent suffering may be an occasion for moral
response and character-building, as Swinburne claims, but why
must innocent suffering possess the enormity that it does? Would
not the divine parent interfere in the quarrels of God's children

if one of them were suffering horribly as a consequence? Swinburne defends God's allowance of extraordinary passive evil in two ways. First, Swinburne counters, God truly sees when passive evil is overwhelming, and God may come to this judgment much less frequently than humans. God may know that "the suffering that A will cause B is not nearly as great as B's screams might suggest to us and will provide (unknown to us) an opportunity to C to help B recover and will thus give C a deep responsibility which he would not otherwise have."[27] Second, God has already placed limits on passive evil in the original act of creation. Swinburne rather coolly observes that "persons live in our world only so many years and the amount which they can suffer at any given time (if mental goings-on are in any way correlated with bodily ones) is limited by their physiology."[28]

These defenses of God's goodness are, at the same time, remarkable denials of innocent suffering's often scandalous proportions and even of its very existence. The first defense suggests that we should be suspicious about conceding that innocent suffering is inordinate for the very reason that God allows it. With this denial, Swinburne transforms innocent suffering into meaningful suffering. The second defense claims that creation includes a built-in protection against extraordinary innocent suffering, namely, death. And so at the very moment that innocent suffering might prove scandalous, Swinburne finds God's goodness in its erasure. In one way or another, then, the best-of-all-possible-worlds theodicy—whether Leibniz's, or Hick's, or Swinburne's—cannot allow innocent suffering to stand and must attribute its transformation, eclipse, or disappearance to the goodness and wisdom of God if that goodness and wisdom are to be logically coherent. We turn now to another kind of theodicy to consider its way of justifying God's goodness before the evil of innocent suffering.

The "Best-of-All-Possible-Gods" Theodicy

The best-of-all-possible-worlds theodicy attends to the actual constitution of the world, evil and all, in its logical defense of God's goodness. What I shall call the "best-of-all-possible-Gods" theodicy revises the classical understanding of God in order to refute any charge of logical inconsistency between God's goodness and the world's evil. Any talk of the "best of all possible" is already a concession to limitation. The best-of-all-possible-worlds theodicy acknowledges the limitations of the world by conceding that both divine and human goodness cannot be what they are apart from a world in which evil really exists. The best-of-all-possible-Gods theodicy is willing to concede a limitation in the divine nature, and thereby relinquish a traditional understanding of God so that God's goodness can still possess coherence before the world's evil.[29] This rubric can be illustrated by any number of process theodicies that are inspired by the philosophical writings of Alfred North Whitehead and Charles Hartshorne. Here, for the purpose of illustration, I shall limit my discussion to the work of David Ray Griffin.

In his book *God, Power, and Evil: A Process Theodicy,* Griffin offers a process account of God's relation to evil.[30] While a best-of-all-possible-worlds theodicy maintains the traditional conception of God's omnipotence and attempts to reconcile that power with God's goodness and the fact of evil, a best-of-all-possible-Gods theodicy gives up the traditional conception of divine omnipotence as inconsistent with the finite and temporal character of reality. God, Griffin claims, is both transcendent and worthy of worship, but is not exempt from the ordinary conditions of existence. God, in Griffin's explanation, possesses remarkable, providential power in the universe that does its utmost to entice individual human lives and all of history toward their best-projected end. God, though, does not possess unlimited power to achieve these ends through the divine will alone.

In Griffin's view, this limitation on divine power does not mean that God lacks perfection. Perfection, conceived traditionally, is the absence of finitude or limitation. God, traditionally conceived, possesses unbounded power, knowledge, goodness, love, and absoluteness in every other virtue that one would want to ascribe to the divine character. Like most process theologians, Griffin sees the traditional conception of divine perfection as one particular strain of historical belief in which the Christian experience of God came to be molded by the intellectual categories of ancient Greek thought.[31] Divine perfection, he insists, can be imagined differently from these assumptions and should not be prejudicially measured by them. Divine perfection is always relative to the world because "according to process thought, there was no beginning of a realm of finite actualities."[32] Both God and the world exist within the conditions of finitude. Within the finite world, Griffin claims, perfect power "must be defined as the greatest power it is conceivable (possible) for a being to have."[33] For God, perfection entails the enjoyment of powers greater than those possessed by any actual being but which, even as perfect, remain within the scope of the limited order. This means "God's power is persuasive, not controlling," and not because "it is better for God to use persuasion, but because it is necessarily the case that God cannot completely control the creatures [of the world]."[34]

This conception of a finitely perfect God has interesting implications for the problem of theodicy. Indeed, the problem of theodicy is the matrix for such a conception of God. If reality is both finite and temporal and the best-of-all-possible-Gods, as the greatest reality, is both finite and temporal, then God faces evil in a finite and temporal way, as do all beings of intelligence in the finite and temporal order. For God, as for human persons, evil is unavoidable, the consequence of moral failure, occasionally transformable by moral strength, insidious, sometimes overwhelming, and encountered as the pain that attends personal sensitivity in a finite, changing world. God, just like humans, is a sufferer before the world's evil. God cannot banish evil from actuality nor prevent its occurrence. Possessing power but lacking omnipotence, God struggles with evil in history, working toward its defeat as every moral person does.

By sketching the portrait of a God who is transcendent but not metaphysically aloof from evil, Griffin is able to ease the tension of the classical dilemma of God's goodness and power in relation to evil. Since the process God is not omnipotent, there is no logical expectation that God's benevolence would counter every possible instance of evil in the universe. Griffin follows most process theologians in affirming divine providence. God's knowledge, goodness, and power work in unity for the benefit of the world. These divine attributes, however, are not eternal. God knows completely how history has transpired but does not know the future. God's goodness is finitely perfect, but neither boundless nor impervious to change. God's power is awesome, but not limitless. These divine qualities all are directed toward the betterment of individual lives, moral communities, and finally history itself, but only by means of persuasion and not through the exercise of absolute power. God stands before evil, so to speak, in much the same manner that virtuous human persons do—in moral commitment born of love, faith, and hope. Yet God's finite perfection enables God to stand before evil in a manner that transcends the disposition of more limited persons. God's wisdom, cultivated through God's full knowledge of the past, is a rich resource for the providential direction of history, and God's capacity to lure the world toward goodness and away from evil is so much greater than the power of any other moral agent.

God suffers with the world, and from within that suffering God struggles ardently, through providential persuasion, to draw good from evil, fulfillment from pain, and virtue from dissolution. In expounding this point, Griffin defends Whitehead's understanding of this cosmic struggle for the good. All that is intrinsically good, he claims, is defined by two criteria: harmony and intensity. Harmony is holistic order, in its grandest proportions the benevolent aim of God for all that is. Intensity is the zealous striving to achieve the divine plan that by its very nature involves risk and hazard. Evil appears in this rather aesthetic conception of goodness as disharmony or aimlessness, on the one hand, and as triviality or complacency, on the other.[35] Meaning in this process worldview is achieved in a relative balance between some present state of harmony and an enacted yearning for still greater harmony. These dynamics of meaning unfold macrocosmically in God's striving ever to bring about the divine plan and microcosmically in the striving of every human life bent on achieving the good. Suffering at the human level issues from one's own moral inertia, from the ways the moral inertia of others wreaks havoc in the human community at large, and from the risks of the divine intensity which, for the sake of the greater good, may have the secondary effect of pain, frustration, loss, and death. Suffering on God's part does not derive from God's own moral inertia, since God has none, but rather from the moral inertia of others and from the divine intensity itself. In Griffin's view, "the risks which God asks the creation to take are also risks for God. Stimulating the world toward greater intensity means the risk that God too will experience more intense suffering."[36]

Is there any place for innocent suffering in this best-of-all-possible-Gods theodicy? My answer to this question requires a number of distinctions that can help us to appreciate this type of theodicy further. A tremendous advantage of the best-of-all-possible-Gods theodicy is its ability to tackle the problem of God's relation to evil while yet acknowledging the existence of innocent suffering. Much human suffering, no doubt, stems from the active evil that sufferers bring about by their own guilty words and deeds. There is nothing in a process worldview, however, that would impute blame to human sufferers of passive evil, and thus explain away innocent suffering. Process theology is not indebted to a traditional myth of the Fall in which guilt becomes an inescapable tragic heritage.[37] Moreover, the suffering that process theologians are willing to attribute to God would seem to be innocent suffering through and through. God's finite perfection would never place God in the position of an evil perpetrator. If moral culpability depends on a malicious intention, then the best-of-all-possible-Gods does no evil, always willing the best possible aim for every individual decision and for all the free decisions of history. God suffers as many of these aims fail to reach fruition and is largely passive before this disharmony and inertia. In fact, God is the paradigmatic innocent sufferer in the assumptions of process thought, for any suffering that God endures is entirely the consequence of the evil enacted by others.

The kind of pathos that God shares with the world precisely *is* innocent suffering. Yet the holistic orientation of this process theodicy has much the same effect on innocent suffering that we observed in the best-of-all-possible-worlds theodicy. We saw that the work of Leibniz, Hick, and Swinburne shared a willingness to make innocent suffering something other than what it is. In one way or another, all three of the best-of-all-possible-worlds theodicists transform innocent suffering into meaningful suffering. They remove the scandalous character of innocent suffering so that its pain, loss, grief, and injustice become resources willed by God for the moral maturation of the sufferer and those in the sufferer's sphere of influence. The best-of-all-possible-Gods theodicy does much the same, though by attending to the divine activity instead of the constitution of the world.

In Griffin's account, the lure of God to nature, to individuals, and to societies is an omnipresent enticement to fulfill the divine aims, though it is in the human realm that response to the divine invitation reaches the sophistication of morality. Innocent suffering, from one point of view, issues from a failure in moral response that spills out into the lives of those now victimized by another's moral inertia. But to the degree that innocent suffering results from the instigation of the divine intensity, it always carries the potential of intrinsic goodness. God beckons the human will to moral response not knowing what the response will be but knowing on the basis of past experience that innocent suffering could result from a particular configuration of the divine intensity. Innocent suffering thus is placed within God's risky purposes, and so within the ambit of divine providence. Even though innocent suffering in any present moment represents the thwarting of the divine aim, its status within the calculation of providence charges it with a meaning that is distinctly theological.

Moreover, innocent suffering, like any actuality in the process worldview, immediately is claimed by the divine will as a resource for a possible providential future. Innocent suffering is an unrealized divine aim yet worth the risk of the divine intensity. Indeed, a finitely perfect God, like an extraordinary chess master, would offer history purposes that already anticipated how the possible losses of innocent suffering could be transformed into the gains of the divine aim. The strongly teleological worldview of process thought enables Griffin's theodicy to make innocent suffering meaningful by investing it with the hope of a moral future that anticipates God's progressive, creative success in the history of cosmic evolution. Just as God has drawn complexity from chaos, life from lifelessness, and intelligence from unintelligent life, so too can the process God cultivate moral gains from innocent suffering, by not allowing innocent suffering to stand as a tragic scandal to divine and human goodness but rather by transforming it immediately into a resource for God's own hopes for history.

In many respects, process theodicy offers an understanding of divine providence that strongly resembles the classical position, at least in its confidence in God's power to draw good from evil. But whereas the classical understanding of providence speaks of God's omnipotent capacity to draw goodness from human guilt and all its suffering consequences in nature and history, process theodicy speaks of God's comprehensive, albeit finite, ability to transform innocent suffering into the meaningful progress of history. In spite of these differences, both the classical and process conceptions of divine providence make extraordinarily strong claims about God's good and loving disposition toward the world. Yet, in spite of their different ways of doing so, the classical and process understandings of providence, just like the best-of-all-possible-worlds theodicy, refuse to allow innocent suffering to stand before God. The classical understanding of providence refuses to acknowledge innocent suffering at all. The process understanding of providence allows innocent suffering to appear for a moment, only to plunge whatever scandal it might pose to divine and human goodness into the depths of God's evolving purposes. Innocent suffering quickly is turned into the prospect of something meaningful.

Innocence and Guilt (Again)

As we can see from the brief presentation above, the modern theodicies sublate innocent suffering in meaning that eclipses the scandal of victimization so that God's goodness can be affirmed on reasonable grounds. The best-of-all-possible-worlds theodicy does so by insisting that suffering falls within the teleology of God's original creative plan. Leibniz tends to conceive of creation's teleology "from above," in the abstract realm of God's infinite knowledge, while Hick and Swinburne tend to conceive of creation's teleology "from below," in the worldly struggles of char-

acter-building. All three best-of-all-possible-worlds theodicists are
unwilling to regard suffering as merely innocent, for doing so
would be an affront to God's unlimited goodness. The best-of-all-
possible-Gods theodicy embraces innocent suffering in the hope
of a better creation that God yet has no absolute power to effect.
As an indirect consequence of the divine intensity, innocent suffering is an ambiguous sign of divine providence and the promise
of goodness yet to come. In some respects, Griffin's God resembles Hick's human agent, raised from the struggling teleology of
the individual life to a struggling teleology of cosmic proportions.
In both types of theodicy, the scandal of innocent suffering is
eclipsed by God's providential aims either in creating the world
as it is or in urging it to be what it might become.

Along with the premodern and the postmodern denials of
innocent suffering, we have in theodicy, then, a third form of
denial that I shall refer to as "modern," since theodicies histori-
cally have been a modern project reflecting the modern confidence in reason. All three forms of denial view innocent suffering
as inconsistent with the goodness of God. Each in its own way
refuses to let innocent suffering remain what it is, regarding it
instead as guilty responsibility (premodern), as statistically
expected misfortune distant from the divine concern (postmodern), or as the grist of teleological struggle for God's moral mill
(modern). As committed as these denials may be to the goodness
of God, their willingness to subvert the integrity of innocent suffering, even for what they judge to be a higher purpose, is extraordinarily problematic. The presence of innocent suffering in
individual lives and in the tragic events of history is so compelling
that its denial can seem fantastic, callous, or an act of evil in its
own right.[38] However much the ancient doctrines, revisionist theology, and the modern theodicies strive to defend God's goodness, their efforts will be unappreciated and even castigated by
Jobian sensibilities, by reasoning not caught in the horns of the
dilemma of divine goodness and power, and, of course, by the
simplest emotional response to innocent suffering wherever it
appears.

Thus far my presentation has considered the evidence of Jewish and Christian doctrine, one kind of postmodern theological

interpretation, and the arguments of some modern philosophers. In the following chapters, I shall attempt to reflect theologically on God's relation to evil in a way that affirms the integrity of innocent suffering. In doing so, I turn my attention specifically to the beliefs of the Christian tradition. First, however, we must again explore the character of innocence and guilt in the personal realm, since these categories will prove crucial to the theological proposal advanced in the pages to come.

At the close of the previous chapter, I described innocence and guilt as moral, ontological, and psychological states that persons occupy in their expected relationship of responsibility to each other. Human persons may be innocent or guilty in the midst of suffering by virtue of their responsibility to the suffering of each other and for the suffering of each other. Since God is affirmed as personal in Christian belief, God too dwells in the network of personal relations characterized by innocence and guilt. Moreover, the traditional beliefs in God's omnipotence and omnipresence mean that God's personal power could extend to suffering beyond the effective power of the human will, such as the suffering caused by natural disaster, illness, or old age.

One might say that God's omnipotence and omnipresence raise the stakes for God's own innocent or guilty relations toward human persons. It is in response to the higher stakes of God's personal relationship to human persons that the premodern, modern, and postmodern denials of innocent suffering take their positions in defense of God's goodness. For if innocent suffering exists in a realm of possible divine action, then divine goodness can be maintained only by denying divine goodness and postulating God's guilt. Unwilling to accept this alternative, the premodern position denies innocent suffering by regarding all human persons as guilty before God; the modern position denies innocent suffering by rendering it meaningful within God's creative providence; and the postmodern position denies innocent suffering before God by removing God's personal, providential presence from natural suffering, thus rendering such suffering amoral, neither innocent nor guilty.

All three forms of this denial, then, respond to a consistent assumption about God's relation to evil: that the presence of innocent suffering in a realm to which God too is present—at most any innocent suffering and at least innocent suffering through natural causes—can be resolved only by postulating God's guilt. Although all three approaches I have considered thus far avoid the Scylla of a guilty God, all fall prey to the Charybdis of denying the common human experience of innocent suffering. By contrast, the approach that I shall develop affirms the reality of innocent suffering, both innocent suffering caused by the human will and innocent suffering that results from natural causes. This affirmation need not entail God's guilt before such innocent suffering, if the offense of evil is approached theologically within a range of reflective options offered by Christian belief. I shall turn to these Christian options in subsequent chapters. At this point, we must consider how God's status in the realm of personal relations might be conceived so that both innocent suffering and God's goodness can be affirmed without compromising either.

Traditional Christian belief in God's providence does not restrict God's graceful, saving presence to all creation. God's goodness is omnipresent, and omnipresent in a manner that communicates the divine omnipotence. God's power extends over all of creation absolutely, and that power is absolutely good. By depicting the God–world relationship in this way, I am not suggesting that God's omnipresence and omnipotence overwhelm human free choice. The Christian tradition allows for the activity of free choice within the province of divine power, particularly the power of grace. However the relationship between nature and grace is conceived, it traditionally assumes the absoluteness of divine power and presence which both the postmodern position and the best-of-all-possible-Gods theodicy deny, largely for the sake of defending God's goodness. But this denial proves unacceptable for the more traditionally minded account of God's relation to evil that I shall develop in the pages to come, at least with respect to God's transcendence and immanence.

In a godless world, or in a world governed only by the most general and distant exercise of divine providence, innocent suffering exists only in the relations between and among human persons. The moral culpability of one person could lead to the innocent suffering of others, as the culpable fail in their moral responsibility and their victims suffer disproportionately to any fault of their own. The victim alone, however, does not make the judgment that innocent suffering has occurred, in a lonely cry of lament. Rather, the context in which innocence and guilt appear as moral, ontological, and psychological states is one in which a community of personal witnesses appropriately joins the victim in attesting to the innocence of his or her suffering, and, we might say as well, attests to the guilt the perpetrator has incurred. In a world in which God is absent, innocence and guilt describe such attested states judged solely by the values constructed in and by moral communities. The claims of faith, however, affirm the existence of a God whose absolute goodness measures all canons of virtue and justice, and whose providential presence could be conceived of as an infinite witness to the innocent suffering that stems from moral guilt in the community of innocent persons. This conception of divine presence widens the scope of God's traditional relation to suffering. Premodern Christian doctrine conceives of God's omnipresence both as judgment on human guilt in a fallen world devoid of innocent suffering and as providence disposed toward the healing of the suffering that issues from human guilt. Conceiving of the divine presence too as a living witness to the injustice of innocent suffering would acknowledge a dimension of human suffering that the premodern position denies and articulate a dimension of providence that the premodern position could not begin to imagine.

This same understanding of God's witnessing presence to innocence can be applied to natural suffering. Typically, innocent suffering is removed from the world of natural causes, either because it is attributed to divine retribution, which in turn renders natural suffering guilty, or because natural suffering is removed from the realm of intentional action, whether human or divine, rendering it amoral, neither guilty nor innocent. Both options assume that talk of guilt or innocence only makes sense in the sphere of personal agency. Natural suffering as divine retribution presupposes the personal agency of human sinners. Natural suffering in the context of divine indifference or absence is neither innocent nor guilty, since it lies beyond the personal agency of both the divine person and human persons. Innocence, so conceived, can only be what it is if *someone* is a guilty perpetrator. Were we, though, to make the category of moral presence rather than the category of moral agency a condition of innocent suffering, a path would open for speaking both anthropologically and theologically of innocent, natural suffering. On this view, the presence of a community of human witnesses itself could provide sufficient condition for innocent, natural suffering, even in the absence of a personal cause for such suffering. Such witnessing presence could not be a vacant, lifeless voyeurism. Only persons in sympathetic solidarity with the sufferer could make the judgment of innocence, a communal judgment in which the sufferer could also share. It would be important for believers to understand God's presence too as a witness to innocent suffering, for within the circle of faith God's personal presence is the indispensable condition for the possibility of moral community, for caring solidarity, and—however untraditional the thought—for innocent suffering inflicted by human perpetrators or by natural causes.

The premodern, modern, and postmodern denials of innocent suffering all negotiate the thorny issue of God's power over the natural forces that cause suffering. The ancient doctrines of covenant and original sin find God's retributive justice in the suffering caused by nature. The best-of-all-possible-worlds theodicy transforms innocent suffering into meaningful suffering by appealing to the wisdom of God's original, creative power. The best-of-all-possible-Gods theodicy reduces God's traditional power, allowing God to coax something better from natural evil without being responsible for it. The postmodern position affirms God's power over creation at large, while removing its providential responsibility from the vagaries of individual suffering. Each position obscures innocent suffering in a certain exercise of divine power rather than allowing it to stand in painful juxtaposition to God's uncompromising goodness. While human persons alone are responsible for moral evil in a godless world, natural suffering always runs the risk of being God's moral evil in a divinely governed world. The premodern, modern, and postmodern positions all skirt this risk by subverting the integrity of innocent suffering in the face of God's power, however it is benevolently exercised.

A more effective approach to God's relation to evil would highlight God's presence and conceive of divine power as a graceful function of that presence. Presence could be construed along these lines much in the manner of God's witness to the innocent suffering caused by the human will, namely, as a witness to the scandal of victimization, which provides a standard for the moral witness of human communities. Here, though, in the realm of natural suffering, where no human will holds sway over natural disaster, disease, and death, and precisely where God's omnipotence in some abstract exercise could have such power, God's presence becomes an affirmation of innocent suffering, and more, a way of naming its evil amidst the larger community of moral witness. Indeed, in the setting of belief one might say that God's moral presence to innocent suffering from natural causes is necessary if such suffering is to be judged evil, and not simply a statistical eventuality or an inevitable consequence of the human condition. If God's witnessing presence to naturally caused innocent suffering is not affirmed, then such suffering is either denied or surrendered to the fates of ill fortune.

Of course, the traditional conception of God's witnessing presence to naturally caused suffering has led to the denial of innocent suffering and to the belief that God causes suffering and death as a just response to human guilt. It is not difficult to see why this has been so. If God were providentially present to naturally caused suffering that was nevertheless judged to be innocent, then the evil of such innocent suffering would have no personal cause.

There are clearly fewer difficulties in imagining God's moral witness to innocent suffering perpetrated by guilty human action. In this scenario, the incorporation of innocent suffering into God's relation to evil may be anomalous, but at least such a relationship aligns innocent effect with guilty personal cause. The conception of God's presence as witness to and affirmation of naturally caused innocent suffering would posit the evil of innocent suffering without a guilty perpetrator, for nature lacks the personal character required for either guilty or innocent agency, humanity's power is insufficient to be the guilty perpetrator of natural evil, and God, I shall argue in the pages to follow, is not the cause of any suffering.

My argument, then, will proceed by holding together three assumptions that are regarded as incompatible by the premodern, modern, and postmodern denials of innocent suffering. First, my account of God's relation to evil affirms a traditional understanding of God's eternity, and with it the absoluteness of all the divine perfections. Among these, the attributes of goodness, power, and presence are especially important for the issues at hand. Thus, I shall hold fast to the traditional Christian beliefs in God's absolute goodness, God's omnipotence, and God's omnipresence, and shall assume with the tradition that these divine attributes all serve God's unlimited providence. Second, my account of God's relation to evil does not deny the integrity of innocent suffering either by attributing all suffering to human guilt as does the premodern view, or by transforming innocent suffering into a meaningful means of moral development, as does the modern view, or by removing innocent suffering from the scope of divine providence, as does the postmodern view. Indeed, my account of God's relation to evil will not deny innocent suffering in any way whatsoever, but instead will follow the conclusions of my first chapter by insisting that the injustice of innocent suffering is an undeniable and tragic moral fact of life. Third, my account of God's relation to evil will reject the view that God is the cause of suffering either by permitting the evil victimization of some by others, or by willing suffering through natural means, including the limitations of the human condition such as disease, old age, and death. Indeed, I shall argue that God neither permits, nor wills, nor causes any kind of suffering or death at all.

Each of the three ways of denying innocent suffering balks at such a configuration of assumptions. The premodern position affirms the first assumption of a traditional conception of God, but denies the second and third assumptions, respectively, that innocent suffering exists and that God is not the cause of suffering and death. The modern position in the best-of-all-possible-worlds theodicy similarly affirms the first assumption and denies the second and third, while the modern position in the best-of-all-possible-Gods theodicy denies the first two assumptions while affirming the third. The postmodern position denies the first two assumptions and, by denying a providence that extends to individual human lives, ignores the third. All three approaches overlap in their rejection of the second assumption, namely, that innocent suffering possesses an undeniable integrity. Let us now consider how these three assumptions, which the established theological and philosophical traditions have found to be incompatible, can be affirmed side by side to account for God's relation to evil.

Notes

1. David Hume, *Dialogues Concerning Natural Religion* (New York: Hafner, 1969), 66.

2. Contemporary works on the philosophy of religion often regard the theological reflections of Augustine and Aquinas on the relationship between God and evil to constitute a mainline Christian position on this matter, which is then termed a "theodicy." See, for example, Barry L. Whitney, *What Are They Saying About God and Evil?* (New York: Paulist Press, 1989), 29–37. For other examples, see the works of John Hick and David Ray Griffin cited later in this chapter. I reserve the term "theodicy" to describe the philosophical defense of God's goodness in the face of evil, a defense that unfolds through rational explanation unconstrained by the authority of scripture and tradition. I would not be inclined, then, to portray Augustine's and Aquinas's reflections on God and evil as theodicies, since these thinkers understand theological reasoning to be responsible to revelation. A theodicy is interested in the claims of faith, but evaluates them by giving priority to the authority of reason, which Augustine and Aquinas do not. A theology is interested in the claims of reason, but evaluates them by giving priority to the authority of revelation and its reception in faith.

3. Barry Whitney details the spectrum of possible theodicies in the thematic divisions to his comprehensive bibliography of publications on this topic. See Barry L. Whitney, *Theodicy: An Annotated Bibliography on the Problem of Evil, 1960–1991* (Bowling Green, Ind.: Bowling Green State University Press, 1998).

4. G. W. Leibniz, "Summary of the Controversy Reduced to Formal Arguments," in *Theodicy: Essays on the Goodness of God, the Freedom of Man and the Origin of Evil,* trans. E. M. Huggard (London: Routledge & Kegan Paul, 1952), 377.

5. Leibniz, *Theodicy*, 253, par. 201.

6. Ibid.

7. Ibid., 267–68, par. 225.

8. Ibid., 268, par. 225.

9. Leibniz, "Summary of the Controversy Reduced to Formal Arguments," 378.

10. Ibid., 385.

11. John Hick, *Evil and the God of Love*, rev. ed. (San Francisco: Harper & Row, 1978), 154.

12. Ibid., 160–66.

13. Ibid., 254.

14. Ibid., 255.

15. Ibid., 255, 256.

16. Ibid., 256.

17. Here Hick criticizes the well-known antitheodicist arguments developed by David Hume. See David Hume, *Dialogues Concerning Natural Religion*, 71–73 (Part XI).

18. Hick, *Evil and the God of Love*, 257.

19. Ibid.

20. Paul Ricoeur proposes such a rhetoric of evil in which "blame" is the language of guilt and "lament" is the language of innocence. See Paul Ricoeur, "Evil, a Challenge to Philosophy and Theology," in *Figuring the Sacred: Religion, Narrative, and Imagination*, ed. M. Wallace, trans. D. Pellauer (Minneapolis: Fortress Press, 1995), 249–61.

21. Hick, *Evil and the God of Love*, 335–36.

22. Richard Swinburne, "The Problem of Evil," in *Reason and Religion*, ed. S. C. Brown (Ithaca, N.Y.: Cornell University Press, 1977), 82, n. 2.

23. Ibid., 84–85.

24. Ibid., 87.

25. Ibid.

26. Ibid., 88.

27. Ibid., 92.

28. Ibid., 89.

29. I concede that my penchant for a consistency in the rubrics "best-of-all-possible-worlds" and "best-of-all-possible-Gods" might disguise a formal difference between them. Both types of theodicy do share a concession to limitation in accounting for God's relation to evil. Talk of the "best-of-all-possible-worlds" configures this limitation as the one, best possible world, evil and all, created by God from among the infinitely possible worlds accessible to the divine imagination. Process theologians would be suspicious of the rubric of "best-of-all-possible-Gods" since it might suggest either that the process God is the best

among possibly imaginable Gods or that the process God is being measured against the classical notion of divine eternity. In the judgment of
many process theologians, the process conception of a God in time is
not one, viable notion of the divine among other possible conceptions
but a logically necessary idea. The process God is indeed limited, but
limitation is the order of reality in the process worldview. Process theologians thus would consider the process conception of God to be logically coherent in its insistence on divine limitation and would reject any
attempt to measure the process conception by the standard of the classical conception.

30. David Ray Griffin, *God, Power, and Evil: A Process Theodicy*
(Philadelphia: Westminster Press, 1976). Griffin has written a sequel to
this work in which he answers his critics. See David Ray Griffin, *Evil
Revisited: Responses and Reconsiderations* (Albany: State University of New
York Press, 1991). I do not find a qualification or clarification in this
later work that addresses my criticism of the process theodicy represented by Griffin's work.

31. Ibid., 257–58.

32. Ibid., 285.

33. Ibid., 268.

34. Ibid., 276.

35. Ibid., 282–83.

36. Ibid., 309.

37. For a process theological reconstruction of the doctrine of original sin, see Marjorie Hewitt Suchocki, *The Fall to Violence: Original Sin
in Relational Theology* (New York: Continuum, 1994).

38. The judgment that the construction of theodicies may itself be
an evil act is developed in Terrence W. Tilley, *The Evils of Theodicy* (Wash-
ington, D.C: Georgetown University Press, 1990).

~ 3 ~

God, Death,
and Innocence

MY GOAL IN THESE PAGES is not to construct a theodicy, a rational defense of God's goodness in the face of evil. I shall not argue for a logical reconciliation of God and evil that satisfies the most rigorous standards of analytical reasoning. Theodicies speak up for God, at least in their willingness to defend God before any blame for the world's suffering. While recognizing the theodicist's good intentions, we would do well to remember God's own judgment on those most ancient theodicists, Job's friends. To Eliphaz the Temanite, who like his compatriots rationalized God's innocence, God said: "My wrath is kindled against you and against your two friends; for you have not spoken of me what is right, as my servant Job has done. . . . [A]nd my servant Job shall pray for you, for I will accept his prayer not to deal with you according to your folly" (Job 42:7–8). Here I shall make every effort to avoid the rationalistic folly of theodicy by approaching the problem of evil *theologically*. Theology draws on the power of reasoning in offering its interpretive insights, but does not make the theodicist's formal logic its path to wisdom. Instead, theology finds its norms in scripture and tradition, which are, for Christian believers, the modes in which the truthful Word of God is revealed.

Drawing this distinction between theodicy and theology, and reading the book of Job in such a way that theodicy is judged to be folly, should not suggest that theology is exempt from the same judgment. Theology may have an advantage over theodicy in its commitment to God's revealed truth in scripture and tradition as the authoritative standard of its interpretive endeavors. Yet, even with revealed wisdom as its guide, theology easily goes wrong in its efforts to bring understanding to faith. Erring, even to the point of folly, becomes more likely whenever a theology risks an interpretation that breaks with customary assumptions about how the claims of scripture and tradition should be represented.

The interpretive course charted thus far risks a reading of scripture and tradition that breaks with customary assumptions. With the premodern account of God's relation to evil, I shall affirm the traditional conception of God's eternity and the absolute perfection of the divine attributes, including omnipotence and omnipresence. But unlike the premodern account of God's relation to evil, I shall not deny the innocent suffering of human persons in order to absolve God of guilt as the direct or indirect perpetrator of suffering. Moreover, I shall refuse to follow the premodern account in placing death, and with it all of human suffering, within God's retributive purposes. As noted in the previous chapter, I shall proceed from the rather uncustomary premise that God neither permits, nor wills, nor causes any kind of suffering at all, and shall attempt to explain how this position can be reconciled with the traditional belief in God's omnipotence, a belief with a wide currency in the community of faith.

Whether the understanding of God's relation to evil presented here errs, and errs to the point of folly, is a judgment that the reader may very well make as the final page is turned. But lest a final negative judgment be stirred somewhat by the disappointment of unreasonably high expectations, it might be helpful at this point to state what my study will *not* do. My account will not "solve" the age-old problem of God's relation to evil. Theodicies venture a comprehensive solution by doing their rational best to render the problem of evil unproblematic. My theological approach moves instead within faith's commitment to scripture and tradition in order to frame a Christian response to the prevalence of evil to the human condition. It does not offer an exhaustive, reasonable solution to a problem since it does not assume there is a problem that needs to be solved only by critical analysis or reflection. Rather, a theological approach maintains that there are a number of consistent ways to configure the assumptions of scripture and tradition to account for the Christian claim that God redresses the evil of the world.

Yet, within this pluralism of consistent and even traditional explanations, there are some that are more and some that are less adequate. This chapter and those that follow argue that a more adequate account of God's relation to evil is one that affirms innocent suffering while holding to the traditional beliefs in God's omnipotence and omnipresence. This argument proceeds from the judgment that the premodern, modern, and postmodern accounts all fall short in their representation of God's relation to evil precisely because each in its own way is unwilling to maintain a traditional understanding of divine providence that allows innocent suffering to stand as a moral fact in human lives.

Arguing for a kind of congruence between a traditional doctrine of divine providence and the moral fact of innocent suffering does not prove threatening to the modern and postmodern accounts of God's relation to evil. These more recent approaches to the issue of God and evil simply disagree with such a proposal by denying the scandalous character of innocent suffering before God, and in the case of the postmodern account and process theodicy, the traditional doctrine of divine providence as well. The modern and postmodern approaches recognize no claim to authority except the cogency of the better argument. But affirming a congruence between a traditional doctrine of divine providence and the reality of innocent suffering does prove threatening to the premodern account of God's relation to evil. Arguing from the authority of scripture and tradition, as I shall, while yet proposing a novel way of configuring their assumptions, poses a challenge to any expectation that good theology is to be a simple reiteration of customary interpretations of scripture and tradition. Good theology throughout Christian history, however, has always found ways to support the authority of tradition by risking novel configurations of its assumptions that still were faithful to its ancient claims. This is a creative standard to which I shall aspire.

My theological proposal will have consequences for understanding a number of traditional doctrines—not only the doctrine
of God but also the doctrines of Christ's saving work, Christian
discipleship, and original sin. The doctrine of God, though, is
clearly at the heart of my theological proposal. The theological
reconstruction of God's relation to evil proposed here shapes the
interpretation of the other doctrines explored in our study. Let us
begin our discussion, then, by considering the two compelling
accounts of God's relation to evil that have flourished in Christian belief.

Death and Divine Power:
The Legal and Providential Explanations

Innocent suffering is unjust suffering. In secular, legal terms, justice or injustice may only be assessed in a context of human
actions that either abide by or violate the law. Those who share
the values of a particular legal system find an ethical touchstone
in its most basic judgments about guilt and innocence. There is
an abiding moral stability in the judgments that the violator of
the law has acted unjustly and so is guilty; that the upholder of the
law has acted justly and so is not guilty; and that the person victimized by the actions of the violator has suffered innocently.
Modern legal explanation, though, accounts for the workings of
justice and injustice—and so innocence and guilt—"from below,"
so to speak. The law regulates human actions and their social consequences. God does not enter into the legal explanations of
responsibility, guilt, and innocence. Even though the law is often
ambiguously applied, its written formulation and history of precedents provide a relative clarity on which the consistent application
of the law depends. Unsurprisingly, in light of this clarity, traditional theology has employed legal explanations to account for
the exercise of God's power and providence.

As we saw in chapter 1, Paul's influential reading of the Genesis story of Adam and Eve interpreted death as divine punishment for the primal sin of the first parents, inescapably imitated
with deathly consequences in every human life. For Paul and for

the Christian tradition that embraced his view as authoritative doctrine, death is God's retribution for the violation of the divine law. Death marks every human being as guilty, as a perpetrator of evil. Humanly fashioned canons of justice or ordinary ethical sensibility might regard human innocence and innocent suffering as undeniable human dispositions. The theological tradition, though, finally denies the integrity of any human innocence, since the possibility of such a moral posture is subverted by the retributive judgment of death. As Augustine notes in *On Free Choice of the Will*, the judgment of death appears to be evil to those who suffer it but in reality this divine punishment is actually just and good, issuing as it does from the justice and goodness of God's own divine will.

This understanding of death as retribution for human evil might harmonize with experience if one attended only to the evil acts accomplished in the course of any life, and especially if one attended only to the viciously evil acts that some persons do often. But most lives are not strictly evil. They are an ambiguous blend of good and evil, virtue and vice, guilt and innocence. Within this moral ambiguity of character, the claims that innocence possesses no standing at all and that death, in any form, is proportionate punishment for unfaithfulness to God seem to lack the very proportion that they are supposed to represent. Moreover, experience testifies that innocent suffering is the most dramatic symptom of evil. Like all forms of evil, innocent suffering, even when it is not suffering to the point of death, brings the presence of death into the midst of life where death's awful power as physical and emotional suffering is utterly disproportionate to personal culpability. The denial of innocent suffering also denies the shocking witness of innocent suffering to the blatancy of evil amidst all its more subtle forms. The result is a kind of homogenizing of evil, as all evil acts now become but a single manifestation of the primordial, evil act of rebellion against God, for which death is then taken to be a just punishment.

We have already seen the theological advantage that this denial of innocent suffering gains in Christian belief. If human guilt is so complete that it eclipses human innocence, then God cannot be regarded as complicit in evil at all. Furthermore, if death and human suffering are the righteous punishment of human sin, then, as symptoms of evil in all its forms, they are expressions of divine justice rather than the divine injustice that one might otherwise judge them to be.

Of course, there is another way in which Christian belief makes death meaningful. Whereas the legal explanation makes death into meaningful justice by placing death and suffering under the divine wrath, popular Christian belief often makes death meaningful by placing it under the divine love. According to this belief, encounters with evil, suffering, and death, while not losing their retributive quality, are yet also occasions for divine providence. Evil, suffering, and death from this perspective convey the power of God's providence to rescue good from evil, to wrest purpose from suffering, and to impose divine mercy and wise foresight on the circumstances and timeliness of death. One finds an excellent example of this emotional response in Oscar Hijuelos's novel *Mr. Ives' Christmas.* In Hijuelos's plot, Edward Ives, a good man, loses his seventeen-year-old son, Robert, to a capricious act of violence. Only days before he was to have entered the seminary to study for the priesthood, the young man is gunned down on a street corner by a teen-aged stranger who, without reason, empties a pistol into his body. The novel traces Ives's lifelong grief as he tries to come to grips with his son's death. In the tragic death scene itself, Hijuelos captures the typical providential explanation of such loss by considering the public reaction to the terrible event. Although Ives is unwilling to speak to the press about his loss, one bystander gave voice to the popular religious explanation: "But they managed to get a quote from one of the local priests, and this was used as a headline in two of the papers: GOD HAS CALLED HIM TO HEAVEN."[1]

There are many variations on this theme of God's goodness at work in the midst of suffering and death. Whether they explain encounters with evil, suffering, and death as purposeful exercises of the divine will in death itself, or find some divine message, instruction, or moral test in suffering, or regard suffering or loss as divinely willed occasions for spiritual growth, they all subsume evil, suffering, and death under God's providential design. This providential explanation does not have the doctrinal status of the

legal explanation, especially in the form of the traditional doctrine of original sin. But in popular belief and practice, the providential explanation fills up the tragic dimensions of the legal
explanation, finding in the often brutal circumstances of suffering the comfort of divine love, mercy, and design. In many
respects, the providential explanation of evil is an indirect
acknowledgment of the very innocent suffering that the traditional doctrine of original sin denies. The providential explanation ascribes God's purposes to suffering in order to acknowledge
an innocence on the part of the sufferer forbidden by the legal
explanation. It tempers the divine wrath by uncovering a benevolent design within the divine judgment. Suffering and death thus
become the divine plan as well as divine punishment.

It may seem strange that God's relation to death could be
described in such contradictory ways at once. On the one hand,
death appears in Christian belief as God's rightful punishment of
the evil that all do and as an expression of the divine wrath; on
the other hand, death appears as God's caring plan—however mysterious it may be—and as an expression of the divine love. Yet, in
religious discourse, it is not unusual to find faithful logic following both the path of official doctrine, as it does in the case of the
legal explanation, and the path of popular, sympathetic emotion,
as it does in the case of the providential explanation, even though
these paths cross and diverge as accounts of God's intention with
regard to death.

As different as these explanations are, however, it is important
to see that they share something very basic. Both explanations
make death a consequence of the divine power. Simply put, God
does death in both explanations. God makes death happen. This
is not to say that God desires death in either account. In the legal
explanation, death is God's just punishment for sin, though not at
all a punishment God is pleased to administer. In the providential
explanation, God desires only to soften the blow of death by
enveloping its time and circumstances in a purposeful and loving
design. In both explanations, though, God's omnipotent causality
brings about death. Although God does not desire death, one
could rightly say that God wills death, at least in the sense that
God's will brings it about, and does so as both justice and mercy.

Throughout the Christian tradition, these have been the two ways in which God's relation to evil has been negotiated. Death, and the seemingly unlimited spectrum of suffering associated with it, is the consequence of human evil and God's just recompense for sin. At the same time, death, even in the most capriciously and viciously evil circumstances like those depicted in the Hijuelos novel, can be filled out by divine purpose so that a providential design eclipses the divine punishment. The legal and providential explanations work hand in hand to negotiate God's relation to evil. The legal explanation protects God's innocence by denying human innocence. The providential explanation puts God's power to work in a way that implicitly acknowledges innocent human suffering. The doctrinal authority of the legal explanation keeps that implicit acknowledgment from becoming explicit since an explicit acknowledgment of innocent suffering would run the risk of God's responsibility for guiltless suffering, that is, evil itself. And yet, even though sublated by official religious teaching, the providential explanation persists in popular belief as a meaningful way of transforming divine punishment into a divine love, a change that could occur only if an unqualified human guiltiness broke before the recognition of at least some degree of human innocence.

Emotional Problems

As prevalent as the providential explanation is as a way of soothing the unrelenting guilt placed on humanity in the legal explanation, it is important for us to note that it presents significant difficulties of its own. The providential explanation may implicitly acknowledge human innocence by wrapping suffering and death in God's omnipotent and omniscient design. Yet, in so many circumstances, the consequence of this explanation is a divine plan that is itself complicit in suffering and death. Once again, the tragic scene cited earlier from the Hijuelos novel illustrates this point.

Upon learning of Robert's death, Edward Ives suffers his grief without public comment, in spite of a public clamoring for response in the face of his son's very public death. The novel's plot catalogues Ives's struggle to deal with the ambiguity, the emptiness, and the heartache of his grief, a grief that is resistant to any easy explanation. Ives stands above the cynicism or despair that this event might cause in his life. He genuinely searches every avenue of meaning that life might offer in order to find meaning in his son's death. Yet, in spite of the reconciliation he achieves with his son's murderer years after the event and the comfort he occasionally finds in the liturgy and symbols of his Catholic faith, Ives sadly discovers that his best efforts fail to rescue any real meaning from Robert's death. His loss refuses to be assuaged by any talk, his own or another's, that would make his son's death "right," given its already tragic occurrence.

Hijuelos ends the book's terrible death scene with the next morning's sentimental newspaper headline precisely to make this point. The headline—"GOD HAS CALLED HIM TO HEAVEN"—voices one way in which faith might respond to the unacceptability of evil's apparent victory over human innocence. God's providence fills up the evil agency so that even in death God's purposes shine forth. Hijuelos, though, offers the quotation not as a comforting explanation but instead as a shocking affront to the brutal fact of Robert's death. The reader is left to imagine that this sentiment does not soothe Ives's grief. It offends. It does not comfort. It hurts. And we should not think that this offense and hurt derive only from the particularly tragic example of loss in the Hijuelos novel. Whether the providential explanation is offered to make sense of the sudden death of a young son or daughter or to make sense of the expected death of an elderly parent after a long, painful battle with cancer, it stirs the same offense and hurt in many who find its account of God's relation to suffering to be unacceptable. Let us consider the source of this emotional conflict.

It is important to acknowledge at the outset that those who offer this explanation do so with the best of intentions. The providential explanation does not aim to offend or to hurt. It tries to offer consolation in the midst of innocent suffering. It is important to acknowledge too that the popularity of this explanation as an ever-ready companion to the legal explanation stems from the

fact that many do indeed find it consoling. Meaningful explanations of anything endure because they are satisfying, and the
providential explanation has endured for centuries whether as
popular consolation offered in the face of any instance of suffering or as Augustine's sophisticated speculation that the power of
divine love dwells in its capacity to bring good out of evil.

There is no doubting, though, that the providential explanation often has the very effect that Hijuelos attempts to depict
through his juxtaposition of Ives's silent grief and the priest's well-
meaning but offensive account of divine design in Robert's mur-
der. The priest's quoted words are offensive because they usurp
Ives's silence and so his own refusal to comment on his loss. But,
in the sensibilities of many, the words offend not only because
they are spoken at all but also, and even more, in what they say.
The providential explanation may work hard to acknowledge
human innocence in the face of the inescapable guilt charged to
humanity in the legal explanation. Yet that particular kind of
acknowledgment comes at the high price of God's willing death.
Moreover, the death God wills in the providential explanation is
not a sweeping judgment of justice on an inescapably sinful
humanity. Instead, the providential explanation imagines that
God reaches into history, into an individual human life, and wills
its suffering and death, which now are attributed to God's loving
will.

Such an explanation, of course, would only be offered by and
for a believer already committed to trust in a providential God.
One would find this account comforting only if one had the
believing capacity to reconcile suffering and death, on the one
hand, and God's providential will, on the other. Certainly, there
is a kind of faith that is capable of this reconciliation, as the
endurance of the providential explanation testifies. And yet, as in
the case of the fictional character of Ives and many nonfictional
believers, there is a kind of faith that finds this explanation emotionally troubling, and even contrary to the most basic claims one
would make about God's relation to evil. Claiming that God's will
is the agency of suffering and death may be consistent with a traditional affirmation of divine omnipotence. But this particular
consistency can raise the specter of a divine wrath divorced from

divine love. Claiming that God's omnipotent will is mercifully at work in suffering and death may be a way of accommodating the evil of innocent suffering in a way that the legal explanation disallows, namely, by enfolding evil in a consoling divine design rather than in divine punishment. But this accommodation is unacceptable to many believers who find the prospect of God's purposeful willing of death to be utterly at odds with the expectations of faith in how God's providence is disposed toward the world.

It should not be surprising that the Christian tradition associates God's love and God's agency in death so closely. At the heart of the Christian story is the event of Jesus' death on the cross, which from the time of earliest Christian belief has been affirmed as God's sacrificial gift for the salvation of the world. God's love manifests itself most fully in this death, which reconciles sinful humanity to God. Whether as Paul's claim that "Christ died for our sins" (1 Corinthians 15:3), or as the Gospel writers' narrative rendition of Jesus' death within a divinely scripted plot, or as the eleventh-century Anselm of Canterbury's attention to the cross as God's gracious restoration of God's honor diminished by sin, this paradoxical intersection of God's love and Jesus' death has enabled many Christians to find a kind of consistency in the providential explanation's confluence of God's love and God's direct agency in any instance of suffering and death. Yet, as comforting as Christians through the ages have found the Gospel message that God's loving will saved the world in Jesus' unique suffering and death on the cross, the idea that God's will is at work in the circumstances of every instance of suffering and death can be deeply troubling. Unlike Jesus' suffering and death, the suffering and death that fill human history are not paradigmatic. They are not the culminating event in an eternal plot. They do not cause the world's salvation. At best, suffering and death are borne well or even heroically. At worst, suffering and death are empty, senseless, and thoroughly dehumanizing. In either case, imagining God's entry into human lives as the agent of suffering and death fractures any paradoxical unity of God's love and human suffering, the likes of which the creed ascribes to the cross. Instead, those offended and hurt by the providential explanation find a searing emotional contradiction in the thought of a loving agency at work in the terrible human history of suffering and death and, more pointedly, in one's own personal encounter with suffering and death.

One of theology's responsibilities is to take a critical perspective on the doctrinal tradition by pointing out ways in which the conceptualization and practice of basic Christian beliefs may have negative consequences for the life of faith, for the church, and even for history. The emotional dissonance that the providential explanation stirs in some believers may well be a symptom of the need for such a critical exercise of the theological task. For those who are troubled by the theological status quo, the prospect of a better explanation offers a possible coherence, otherwise lacking, among the claims of faith. Theological criticism can also have the unenviable responsibility of explaining to those consoled by a certain belief that its untroubled character *should* be troubling when placed in the larger context of the truthful witness of scripture, tradition, and experience. Those who find comfort in the providential explanation might very well ask why their solace should be disturbed by unwanted criticism, why they too should find the providential explanation to be emotionally problematic. The only acceptable answer is a better explanation of God's relation to suffering and death.

Admittedly, the providential explanation has endured in popular belief through the ages. Its enduring popularity, though, may be much more a product of the Christian tradition's age-old denial of innocent suffering than of any emotional satisfaction inherent in the thought of God's loving agency in death. We have seen that the providential explanation serves as a companion to the legal explanation, ever softening the severity of its authoritative, doctrinal claim that all are guilty, and none are innocent, before God. The providential explanation is an oblique acknowledgment of innocent suffering within a tradition that officially forbids such an acknowledgment. Finally, its affirmation of God's loving purposes at work in the midst of suffering is but a shadow of the traditional claim that such suffering is God's just retribution. What the providential explanation yearns for can never be satisfied consistently within the wider assumptions of the Christian tradition. Given those assumptions, which regard the denial of innocent suffering as the only way to uphold the goodness of God, the desire to affirm innocent suffering before God has no alternative to the providential explanation's very tentative consolation.

A better explanation would begin with the insight that human beings do suffer innocently in a myriad of ways—not only as sheer victims of human hatred and violence but also through natural causes, and not only through natural causes that cause death capriciously and before its time but also in the suffering that attends the most expected death at the end of a long life. The providential explanation indirectly concedes the innocence of such suffering, but only as a qualifier to the legal explanation, and so only as a kind of emotional sop to the commonsense desire to acknowledge innocent suffering. A better explanation—one truer to the undeniable presence of innocent suffering in human experience—would unbridle the desire at work in the providential explanation. Such a theological account would allow innocent suffering to stand on its own terms, apart from the legal explanation and with all its scandalous integrity, and now envision God's presence to such suffering as divine comfort in the midst of human innocence. The providential explanation conceives of God's presence in such circumstances as God's agency in suffering and death, the very cause of the emotional dissonance that many find (and, I would argue, all should find) in this popular Christian belief. A better explanation would deny any agency of God at all in suffering and death. Such a conceptualization would remove God's causality from suffering and death while yet positing God's presence to innocent suffering both as moral witness and, in a traditionally Christian fashion, as the graceful power of salvation.

The obvious advantages of this proposal are twofold: first, it allows the scandal of innocent suffering to be acknowledged directly and thus enables theological explanation to be consistent with the claims of experience; second, it eliminates the source of emotional conflict in the providential explanation by denying a double motivation toward death on God's part. If defensible, these would be remarkable theological gains with extensive pastoral implications. By the same token, this proposal suggests a host of drawbacks that raise deep concerns about its orthodoxy. Limiting God's agency at all seems to deny the traditional doctrine of divine omnipotence that so many believers eagerly affirm. Moreover, the affirmation of an uncompromised human innocence before God, even innocence in the midst of suffering, seems to deny the traditional doctrine of original sin. Such a denial, however qualified, would open the door to Pelagianism by undercutting the utter need for divine grace and so the gratuitousness of salvation. With such results, the affirmation of innocent suffering would show itself to be a disguised human arrogance, the assertion of human autonomy masquerading as powerless, though thoroughly guilty, suffering. Finally, if innocent suffering were allowed to stand before God, then God's guilt before such innocence would seem to be inescapable. The tradition's consistent denial of innocent suffering invests God's infinite goodness in the pervasiveness of human guilt. A theological proposal that made room for innocent suffering within the history of human guilt would seem to compromise God's goodness in a way that would be unacceptable for the life of faith.

These concerns are real and will need to be addressed in the pages that follow. At this point, I offer the judgment that no one of them, or all together, defeats my proposal that God not have any agency in suffering and death so that the evil of innocent suffering may enter the realm of theological explanation. The first step in arguing for this proposal involves showing just how God's agency can be removed from suffering and death while yet continuing to affirm the traditional divine attributes of omnipotence and omnipresence. Since my proposal is a theology and not a theodicy, the authoritative resources of scripture and tradition will guide the reasonable course of this argumentation.

Death and Divine Power: An Alternative Explanation

When believers address the God of the biblical tradition, they give voice to their experience of the divine person. Throughout the Old and New Testaments, the biblical authors consistently name the creator of heaven and earth, the God of Abraham, Isaac, and Jacob, and the same God whom Jesus calls *Abba* as the "living God." There are many examples of this title in scripture. A few will suffice here. The author of the book of Deuteronomy asks rhetorically, "For who is there of all flesh that has heard the voice of the living God speaking out of fire, as we have, and remained alive?" (5:26). Paul extols the dignity of the faithful community by calling it the "temple of the living God" (2 Corinthians 6:14). In the Gospel of Matthew (16:16), Peter identifies Jesus by calling him "the Messiah, the Son of the living God." The author of John's Gospel accentuates the power and authority of the preexistent Christ by identifying his very being with the divine attribute of life: "What has come into being in him was life, and the life was the light of all people" (John 1:3–4). In the same Gospel, the incarnate Christ, ever portraying himself as the manifestation of the Father, testifies, "I am the resurrection and the life" (John 11:25).

Throughout the Bible, this way of naming God conveys the belief that God is a person, and so a God whose self-identity and self-transcendence are the fullness of life. Speaking of God as the living God is also a way of confessing belief in God as the creator of all things, among which are living things that receive their life as a gift from God, the source of all life. The Genesis account (1:26) of the creation of humanity in God's own image and like-ness has been interpreted, of course, in a variety of speculative ways, since its provocative, albeit ambiguous, phrasing seems to hold the key to the meaning of human nature. A modest inter-pretation of the phrase "image and likeness" consistent with the tradition's wider beliefs about God and human beings would understand the words to depict the rich, personal way in which human beings share in the life of God, in however limited a way. The Genesis story portrays personal life as the consummate gift and crowning achievement of God's creative activity. This naming of God as the living God, then, expresses a belief both about the divine nature and about God's creative, providential presence to all life, and, in a special way, to human life. The living God is the God of the living, near to the life-world as a nurturing and com-forting presence. The divine life is also the power of all life, a belief that has interesting implications for the traditional divine attribute of omnipotence.

A common understanding of divine omnipotence conceives of God's power as so unlimited that it is able, in principle, to accomplish any activity and as so extensive that there are no boundaries to its causal influence. There is some biblical and traditional justification for this view. If God, according to Genesis, calls the universe into existence and, in the words of the Nicene Creed, is the "maker of heaven and earth," then all power finally is God's, at least with respect to its origin. Often, though, this simple logic of faith lapses into a formal, philosophical logic, the very kind of reasoning on which theodicies depend. The result is an understanding of omnipotence that makes God's utterly unlimited power a logical problem to be negotiated before the evil of the world. In this philosophical approach, divine omnipotence becomes a premise in a logical conundrum, to be defended and justified in a "best-of-all-possible-worlds" theodicy or denied and reconstructed in a "best-of-all-possible-Gods" theodicy. But if God is the living God and, as the living God, the God of life, then it would be more consistent with the biblical tradition to conceive of God's omnipotence not as a theoretical term in a logical problem but as an actual power exercised creatively in behalf of life wherever life dwells in creation, especially in the personal life that human beings share with God.

Such a focus on omnipotence as God's life-giving and life-promoting power need not restrict divine ability or efficacy, as in a process conception of God. Divine omnipotence can be conceived of primarily as God's life-giving and life-promoting causality without diminishing God's power over creation. As the creator of *all* things, God has and exercises power over the lifeless world too. And since we are interested in sketching a rather traditional theological portrait, we can and should insist that God's omnipotence be conceived of as eternal and as absolutely perfect. The only departure that our life-oriented conception of divine omnipotence makes from common understandings of divine power entails the removal of God's causal agency from death. If God is the living God and the creator of life, then the view that God causes death in any way—even to accomplish some good as the providential explanation holds—is theologically incoherent. How could God, the creator and sustainer of life, be the purveyor of death in any way whatsoever?

Once again, let us recall the tradition's answer to this question. According to Christian belief, God does not cause suffering and death in any way that could be construed as evil. God causes suffering and death retributively, the legal explanation claims, in order to bring divine justice to human sin. God causes certain kinds of suffering and death benignly, the providential explanation claims, so that God's love will coincide with God's justice. Both explanations negotiate the problem of innocent suffering before God: the legal explanation by denying innocent suffering; the providential explanation by indirectly acknowledging innocent suffering even as it confirms the legal explanation's official denial. The legal explanation, in the words of Paul, is God's judgment of "condemnation for all" (Romans 5:18). The providential explanation offers consolation where condemnation alone would otherwise prevail, though the promise of *this* consolation quickly becomes an affront to those who find it comes at the high cost of God's causality in suffering and death. There is, however, an alternative answer to the question of how the Lord of life could be a purveyor of death in any way—an answer that addresses the emotional affront of God's deathly causality by following a different path through scripture and tradition.

Scriptural Evidence

As I begin consideration of the scriptural evidence for an alternative conception of God's relation to death, it is important to acknowledge from the start that the Bible does not offer overwhelming support for my cause. If it did, my explanation would not be an alternative one. The creator God of Genesis is the God of the Old and New Testaments, a God whose power reaches over the entire universe. It seems incongruous to sever divine causality from anything in God's creation, even from death. And yet, to the degree that the power of evil manifests itself as the workings of suffering and death in human life, and the biblical God is the God of life who stands opposed to all evil, there is a real sense in which

the entire scriptural narrative can be enlisted to support the theological judgment that God does not cause death in any way at all.
We may proceed by citing particular scriptural accounts of God's
relation to death that provide some justification for an argument
along these lines.

One of the most moving passages in the Hebrew scriptures is
found in Isaiah 25. The ancient prophet praises the God of Israel
for doing "wonderful things" (Isaiah 25:1) for God's people. God
has been "a refuge to the poor, a refuge to the needy in their dis-
tress." God has provided the people of Israel with "a shelter from
the rainstorm and a shade from the heat," and has stilled "the
song of the ruthless" (25:4, 5). These expressions of faith in divine
providence proceed by speaking not only of what God has done
for Israel but also of what God will do in behalf of all people:

> On this mountain the Lord of hosts will make for all peoples a
> feast of rich food, a feast of well-aged wines, of rich food filled
> with marrow, of well-aged wines strained clear. And he will
> destroy on this mountain the shroud that is cast over all peoples,
> the sheet that is spread over all nations; he will swallow up death
> forever. Then the Lord God will wipe away the tears from all
> faces, and the disgrace of his people he will take away from all
> the earth, for the Lord has spoken. It will be said on that day,
> Lo, this is our God; we have waited for him, so that he might
> save us. This is the Lord for whom we have waited; let us be glad
> and rejoice in his salvation. For the hand of the Lord will rest on
> this mountain. (25:6–10)

This strong statement of hope in God's salvation anticipates the
coming day when God's victory over evil will be final. Isaiah
describes this day as a time of celebration for the reconciliation
that God will bring between enemies, for the end that God will
put to personal failure, and for the joy with which God will shat-
ter the world's sadness. The prophet imagines this day of salvation as the occasion for a sumptuous meal in which all will share,
their sharing a testimony to the communal character of God's victory. The boundless scope accorded in this text to God's saving
power is somewhat unusual. The Jewish tradition more typically
describes God's salvation as a disposition toward Israel, the chosen people of God, as the preponderance of passages in the same

book of Isaiah show. Isaiah 25, however, depicts God's defeat of evil as universal in its proportions. Salvation, in Isaiah's vision, cannot truly be a consummate defeat of evil unless all are beneficiaries of God's goodness.

It is even more unusual that this ancient Jewish text portrays this universality in the way that it does—as God's destruction of all death and of all the suffering that accompanies every encounter with evil. Typically, the Hebrew scriptures envision Yahweh's providence as God's protection of Israel from the aggression of hostile nations. This conception of providence, which was shaped by the actual history of Israel, represents salvation as a national peace and sovereignty beyond the threat of victimizing domination and exile. But Isaiah's prophetic imagination risks more. He conceives the fullest disposition of divine providence as God's swallowing up death forever, almost as though God's portion in the celebratory meal will be the very death that enshrouds all peoples. God's consumption of death is death's destruction for the sake of all who stand under its terrible power. For Isaiah, God's victory extends to death's evil consequences. The suffering too that attends death will be wiped away by God, just as God will wipe away from all faces the tears that issue from the human encounter with evil. Clearly, the text describes an exercise of divine providence that far surpasses a people's hopes for peace and national stability, for Isaiah 25 offers a salvational vision universal in both scope and power.

Whereas ancient Jews would interpret God's defeat of death in Isaiah 25 as a historical event in a much-anticipated future, Christians throughout the ages have read this passage in light of their belief in a resurrected life that God wills for all humanity, a resurrected life that has already broken into history in Jesus' resurrection but that will be fulfilled beyond history in eternal life. The author of the New Testament book of Revelation, for example, presents a Christian understanding of God's defeat of death that relies directly on Isaiah 25:

> Then I saw a new heaven and a new earth; for the first heaven and the first earth had passed away, and the sea was no more. And I saw the holy city, the new Jerusalem, coming down out of heaven from God, prepared as a bride adorned for her husband.

> And I heard a loud voice from the throne saying, "See, the home
> of God is among mortals. He will dwell with them; they will be
> his peoples, and God himself will be with them; he will wipe
> every tear from their eyes. Death will be no more; mourning
> and crying and pain will be no more, for the first things have
> passed away." (Revelation 21:1–4)

This apocalyptic vision places the final victory in a history trans-
figured by God's power, in a renewed and restored existence
made whole by God's destruction of evil. The book of Revelation
sees human history, with all its travails, as the beneficiary of this
saving act of God. Yet finally it understands the graceful life won
by the divine victory to stand in "radical discontinuity"[2] to the life
of suffering and death that preceded it. Although these biblical
writings portray the eschatological scene in somewhat different
ways, both imagine God's saving power put to work in the destruction of death and its insidious hold on human lives.

There is another common element shared by these apocalyptic writings that can serve our theological interest in God's relation to death. Believers in the traditions that hold these texts
sacred do so because they regard them as divine revelation, as
God's revealed word. Jewish and Christian readers of Isaiah
believe that it is God who speaks through the ancient Hebrew
prophet, and Christian readers of Revelation believe that it is God
who speaks to and through the late-first-century author and
visionary who calls himself God's servant, John (Revelation 1:1).
If we approach these writings from within this circle of faith, then
the words of these apocalyptic visions are God's own testimony
about a future that God promises to bring to reality. That God
speaks of death's destruction by making a promise should not be
surprising to Christians who have learned from the Protestant
Reformer Martin Luther. Luther never tired of noting that God's
revealing words in the Bible are presented in two modes of
speech, "law" and "gospel."[3] God's speech as "law" appears in
scripture's ethical commands, like the Ten Commandments (Exodus 20:1–17) and the Sermon on the Mount (Matthew 5–7),
which, Luther assumed, a deeply fallen humanity could never fulfill. God's speech as "gospel" is a promise by which God pledges
the accomplishment of an act. In the speech-mode of gospel or

promise, God conveys the good news that eternal life is a divine gift that will be consummately given to humanity in spite of humanity's utter unworthiness. Divine speech as promise is not only communication but also an act by which God commits God's self to the performance of these words. Simply put, God's promise that humanity will be saved is an utterance that believers are convinced God will make true, given the power and faithfulness of the person who promises.

Luther introduced the law–gospel distinction in order to condemn what he understood to be the Catholic error of salvation by human works and to defend God's complete initiative in salvation by grace alone. In spite of this polemical history, any Christian confession can surely appreciate Luther's insight that the Bible often presents the revelation of God's "good news" in the form of a promise, and that this promise expresses God's loving and unfailing commitment to bring humanity to resurrected, eternal life, an act that only God can accomplish. And were one to read the Bible as a single book, as a canonical whole, then one could argue, as Ronald Thiemann has, that there is a narrative quality to God's promissory language, that the biblical story can be read, from creation to eschaton, as God's narrated promise to cause the world's salvation.[4] Understood in this way, the entire content of scripture is God's unique promise—enacted as it is spoken—to rescue humanity from evil. All of the promises that God makes in scripture are but expressions of this foundational promise to which believers respond in faith.

It is precisely this canonical perspective on the entire Bible as God's narrated and saving promise that can help us to appreciate our earlier scriptural citations on God's relation to death. Understood as divine revelation, the passages we considered in Isaiah and Revelation can be read not merely as words from the mouth of the prophets but as words from the mouth of God. So understood, the divine words lend themselves to being read as promises spoken by the saving God. It is God who promises to swallow up death forever, and God who promises to wipe away the tears from all faces. It is God who promises that death will be no more, and God who promises that mourning and crying and pain will cease. It is God who promises to dwell among mortals, and God who

promises to prepare for all peoples a feast of rich food. Read in
this way, the texts of Isaiah and Revelation are very particular
expressions of a promise that is so woven into the biblical narrative from beginning to end that it could be considered a verbal
dimension of its plot. In narrative perspective, the divine promise
to destroy suffering and death appears everywhere in the Bible,
from every enactment of Yahweh's covenantal promise to Israel to
every word and deed of Jesus that promises and gracefully accomplishes eternal life. The logic of this extended narrative promise
places every word that God speaks on the side of life. Believers
judge these life-affirming words to be trustworthy to the degree
that they have real experience of the God who speaks them. As
Thiemann reminds us, one measures a promise by the character
of the person who makes it.[5] The character of the biblical God,
the God of the living, manifests itself in the creation and sustenance of life, and, in a Christian reading, in a providence that so
treasures life that it brings created life to a share in God's uncreated, eternal life.

Just as this canonical perspective on biblical revelation can
help us to appreciate how the biblical promises extend throughout all of scripture, the particularity of the promise in Isaiah and
Revelation helps us to understand the content of this extended
biblical promise. In both Isaiah and Revelation, God promises in
the most direct of ways to destroy death. This single promise
speaks of the utter finality of God's defeat of death. The passages
in Isaiah and Revelation that have figured so prominently in my
argument are apocalyptic writings. Their faith and hope in God's
victory over evil at the end of the world lead them to accentuate
God's opposition to the death that God will vanquish totally at
the end of time. Although these apocalyptic writings are distinc-
tive as visionary texts rich in symbolism and metaphor, their con-
strual of God's relation to evil is, in many respects, typical of the
entire biblical narrative as a canonical whole. Since the biblical
God is the God of life, it should come as no surprise that this God
would oppose all that is opposed to life. The clarity of this belief
as expressed in Isaiah and Revelation enables us to clarify the
many ways this opposition between God and death appears
throughout the biblical narrative. This opposition appears in the

primordial juxtaposition of the creating God and the waters of chaos in the opening scene in Genesis. It appears in God's liberation of Israel from Pharaoh's enslaving power in Exodus. It appears in God's anger in the face of Israel's repeated faithlessness throughout the Hebrew scriptures. The opposition between God and death appears in Paul's juxtaposition of the "flesh" in which "nothing good dwells" (Romans 7:18) and the spiritual body of the resurrected person, brought by God to "imperishable . . . glory . . . [and] power" (1 Corinthians 15:42–43). It appears in Mark's Christology of Jesus as divine exorcist, engaged in a cosmic battle with the evil spirits who smother life in death. And it appears in John's confident assertion that the life-giving light of the Son of God "shines in the darkness, and the darkness did not overcome it" (John 1:5).

On one level, the Bible's consistent portrayal of God's opposition to death might be understood as an expression of the basic Jewish and Christian belief that God stands opposed to all evil. According to these traditions, God does not do evil. These traditions, though, are often reluctant to identify the evil that God does not do with death, which they ascribe to God's retributive or providential purposes.[6] When death is God's retribution or providence, it is no longer opposed to God but becomes instead an extension of the divine will. In such cases, the biblical opposition between God and evil does not issue in an opposition between God and death. But the specificity of the divine promise in Isaiah and Revelation points us in another direction. Here God's promise to "swallow up death forever" so that "death will be no more" is an invitation to read the narrative theme of opposition not only as one between God and evil but also as an opposition between God and death, so often encountered as evil when it enters human lives.

The very assumptions that attend the rhetoric of promise encourage this identification of evil and death's power over life, and so God's opposition to all death. A promise, Thiemann notes, "is an intentional speech-act by which the speaker assumes an obligation to perform some specified future act on behalf of the hearer."[7] The logic of any promise places both the words and the will of the promiser on the side of the promised action, an action that begins to unfold even with the making of the promise. Authentic promise keeping requires a consistency on the part of the promiser that extends from word to deed. This consistency conveys the very character of the promiser, who works to make the words of promise real in action. Human promises may fail to be realized, frequently as a consequence of faithlessness and betrayal but also when made with the best of intentions and enacted with the most ardent character. Unforeseen circumstances, insurmountable obstacles, or a hope that overreaches its ability to deliver on the words of promise—in short, human limitations—all can prevent human promises from being kept. Christians, however, believe in the omnipotent God whose character defines truth and goodness and whose words bring the universe into existence just by being spoken. God's promise to "swallow up death forever" so that "death will be no more" begins to be enacted with its very utterance and cannot fail to be realized, given the faithfulness and power of the one who makes it.

This unfailing unity between God's promising word and fulfilled deed, which we can conceive of as God's eternal constancy, makes any claim for a causal relation between the divine will and death inconsistent. The logic of God's promise requires that God have a certain disposition toward death. The promise places God at odds with death as the source of the tears that God has pledged to wipe away. God's revealing promise is itself a testimony to the consistency of God's character from spoken word to willed deed. This unity between God's words and acts is at once God's faithfulness to humanity and the graceful cause of human faith in God. Maintaining God's causal relation to death, as the legal and providential explanations do, vitiates this unity in God's steadfast character by introducing a "double" will into God's being according to which God promises the defeat of a death that God has caused. But if God has promised to destroy all death, then how could God be the cause of death in any way? Assuming the integrity of God's biblical promise throughout the entire biblical narrative, how could the efficaciousness of God's own life-giving power be made consistent with the claim that divine intentions cause death, however righteously or purposively? The nature of *this* promise spoken by *this* God, whose power is completely on the side of life, seems to affirm this sensibility of faith expressed so powerfully in the apocryphal Wisdom of Solomon (1:12–14): "Do not invite death by the error of your life, or bring on destruction by the works of your hands; because God did not make death, and he does not delight in the death of the living. For he created all things so that they might exist. . . ." If God does not make death, as the ancient author claims, then God's omnipotence would not cause death, since God's power stands entirely on the side of the life that it has created.

Traditional Evidence

The Christian tradition also offers support for denying God's causality in death. In a famous study entitled *Christus Victor*, Gustav Aulén has explored three understandings of salvation that have flourished in Christian belief.[8] One of these understandings provides an interesting resource for retrieval.

Since the eleventh century, Aulén observes, Christians have been inclined to think of atonement in terms of the theological model proposed by Anselm of Canterbury (c. 1033–1109). In Anselm's view, Jesus' death on the cross is a sacrifice that sets aright the assault on God's honor perpetrated by human sin. Anselm's explanation is a legal one, in which Jesus takes on the penalty that humankind owes God for the violation of the divine law. The cross is the scene of an exchange in which God's honor is restored by a satisfaction that Jesus makes on behalf of a fallen humanity incapable of paying to God the price of reconciliation incurred by sin. Aulén labels this model of atonement the "Latin" type, due to its origin in and popularity throughout the medieval Roman Catholic tradition. Another, far less popular conception of atonement is the "subjective" or "humanistic" model, which Aulén finds in the theology of Peter Abelard, in the spirituality of the Pietists, and in the liberal theologies of Friedrich Schleiermacher and his modern disciples. Here atonement is conceived of as emotional ease in the experience of God, whether as an untroubled religious consciousness or a satisfied moral conscience. Unlike the legal model, which conceives of sin as the human violation of the harmony God has willed for the created order, the

subjective model conceives of sin as human imperfection that yet
might be rectified by human efforts. Although Aulén describes
the aim of his study as "historical, [and] not . . . apologetic,"[9] he
clearly judges the Latin model to be limited and the subjective
model to be fundamentally deficient. The title of Aulén's book
names a third model, against which the shortcomings of the Latin
and subjective models are measured.

Aulén has argued that many of the early Christian writers
shared a particular conception of how God's saving power
achieves its loving ends. The church fathers, who were the tradition's first theologians, conceived of God's salvation as a battle
that raged throughout the entire cosmos. The battle lines in this
conflict are clearly drawn. On one side stands God, the maker of
all things, whose life, goodness, and truth are woven into the fab-
ric of existence. On the other side stands all the evil that permeates and corrupts this same created order. Evil in this model is not
equated with rebellious human actions that violate the divine law,
as it is in the Latin model, or as an only relative state of human
imperfection that might be brought to betterment through
human initiative, as it is in the subjective model. The ancient
fathers conceived of evil as a power that holds sway throughout
the entire universe and by which humanity is completely overwhelmed. This idea of a most formidable evil, Aulén notes, often
appears in these first theologies as the triadic formula "sin, death,
and the devil."[10] Like the devil, sin and death are here imagined
as objectified powers with lives of their own. Together, sin, death,
and the devil share a single evil agency bent on the destruction of
God's life-giving power, particularly as it dwells in God's human
creatures. Held hostage by forces initially unleashed by Adam's
primal sin but that now supersede any one sinful act or all sinful
acts together, humanity cannot resist these powers by any means
of its own. This ancient understanding of atonement, which
Aulén calls the "dramatic" or "classic" model,[11] sees God's salvation as an engagement of the powers, much in the manner of a
military operation in which Christ appears as God's champion in
the embattled cosmos to destroy evil and release humanity from
its clutches. Although the incarnation is an extraordinary and
decisive intervention in this war between God and evil, the drama

of God's graceful reconciliation of the world continues in the face of the broken, eschatologically defeated, but still powerful forces of sin, death, and the devil.

There are many variations on this dramatic theme of atonement in patristic literature. Aulén cites the work of Irenaeus of Lyons (c. 130–c. 200) as a clear example of the basic motif:

> . . . but through the Second Man [Christ] He [God] bound the strong one, and spoiled his goods, and annihilated death, bringing life to man who had become subject to death. For Adam had become the devil's possession, and the devil held him under his power. . . . Wherefore he who had taken man captive was himself taken captive by God, and man who had been taken captive was set free from the bondage of condemnation.[12]

In an early work, *On the Incarnation of the Word*, Athanasius of Alexandria (296–373) portrays the cross as the battlefield on which the Son of God defeats the forces of Satan: "Whence it was quite fitting that the Lord suffered this death [on the cross]. For thus being lifted up he cleared the air of the malignity both of the devil and of demons of all kinds, as he says: 'I beheld Satan as lightning fall from heaven. . . .'"[13] The late-fourth-century Cappadocian father Gregory of Nyssa (331–393) provides a third example of this conflictual understanding of salvation by suggesting that God wins the battle for the cosmos by offering an incarnational bait to the demonic deceiver:

> . . . the opposing power could not, by its nature, come into immediate contact with God's presence and endure the unveiled sight of him. Hence it was that God, in order to make himself easily accessible to him who sought the ransom for us, veiled himself in our nature. In that way, as it is with greedy fish, he might swallow the Godhead like a fishhook along with the flesh, which was the bait. Thus, when life came to dwell with death and light shone upon darkness, their contraries might vanish away. For it is not in the nature of darkness to endure the presence of light, nor can death exist where life is active.[14]

Modern men and women are not inclined to imagine evil in such a grand, mythological way. Hannah Arendt speaks for modern sensibilities on the nature of evil in judging the all-too-human actions of the Nazi war criminal Adolf Eichmann to be "banal," as insipid and small as they were horrible.[15] Sharing Arendt's judgment that history's horrors are the work of human hands, most modern Christians would find it difficult to think of sin as something other than human frailty before an otherwise resistible desire. Many modern Christians would be even less inclined to portray an encounter with evil as a direct confrontation with a personal demonic being. To the modern believer, neither "sin" nor the "devil" seems to possess the kind of independent agency that they do in the dramatic model. Of the three terms in the triadic formula, though, there is a sense in which "death" still is encountered as a power that seems to have an agency of its own, not as a personified evil spirit but as the inevitable destruction that comes to life and before which all finally stand powerless. Indeed, those inclined to demythologize the ancient idea of atonement would do so by explaining the objective character of evil in its symbolism as a description of the kind of objectivity that death seems to have in human lives. Even if modern Christians do not recognize their worldview in the wider, mythological features of the dramatic theory, the way it defines the relationship between God and death can still be religiously meaningful.

Death enters our lives as an "other," whether through the death of someone close to us, through anonymous deaths for which we feel sympathy, or through the prospect of our own death. Death enters our lives as an "other," whether it comes as a terminal disease early in life, as the consequence of capricious or systemic violence, or as the inevitable end to the slow debilitation of old age. The dramatic theory of atonement accounts for this experience of the otherness of death both in the way it portrays human helplessness in the face of evil's overwhelming power and in the way it sets God against evil as a divine warrior devoted to an enemy's destruction. No doubt, there are aspects of this representation that are not only anachronistic but also counterproductive. Darby Kathleen Ray has noted the ancient model's limitations, even as she commends its contemporary relevance. At its worst, the model can seem to advocate a dualism between God and evil that makes too much of evil's power in the divinely created order. Furthermore, its very appreciation for the otherness of evil can be co-opted to serve the workings of hatred as the differences between persons and peoples are symbolized by the religious imagery of demonic otherness.[16] To Ray's concerns, we can add the model's identification of divine power and military might, which throughout human history has often been used for the most heinous purposes.

Yet, as mythologically unsuited as the ancient model may be for wholesale modern retrieval, its refusal to place God's power on the side of death in any way can provide an authoritative precedent in the patristic tradition for the argument presented here. Indeed, the dramatic theory is so willing to identify evil and death, and thus oppose God and death, that its imagery implies that God is not the cause of death. The model's root metaphor of God's saving, ongoing battle with death for the liberation of humanity implies that death is not only humanity's enemy but also God's, and to ascribe it to God would betray God's own salvational will. Were God aligned even providentially with death, God's own actions would be set over against God's unfailing commitment to destroy death. This, in turn, would postulate a "double will" in God, much in the manner that we saw in our analysis of the scriptural evidence.

We need not follow Aulén in his judgment that the patristic model is the only truly authentic understanding of Christian atonement in order to appreciate its redemptive symbolism.[17] Indeed, if the dramatic theory provides some authoritative warrant for my theological proposal, it does so on the basis of its rather uncustomary claim that God's power is foreign to death, rather than for the authority Aulén ascribes to its unbroken continuity from the New Testament writers, through the church fathers, to Luther. We can continue our discussion of God's relationship to death by considering how this understanding, sanctioned to some degree by scripture and tradition, allows the scandal of innocent suffering to stand before an omnipotent and all-good God.

Where the Evidence Leads

Read together, scripture and tradition offer understandings of God's relation to death that support my theological proposal.

Both distance God from evil, as does any expression of Christian belief. Both the trajectory of scriptural promise set by Isaiah 25 and the dramatic theory of atonement identify evil with death. The conflict between God and evil undercuts any providential alliance between the two. The logic of God's scriptural promise and the battle lines drawn between God and the demonic enemy in the dramatic motif place God's life-giving power so completely against death that any causal relation between the two could only be affirmed by positing a double will in God. Various Christian beliefs and doctrines have entertained the thought of a double will in God. On one end of the spectrum, the providential explanation presents the double will in a popular belief that mingles God's retribution and blessing in a single, divine act. On the other end of the spectrum, the double will appears occasionally in Christian teaching as the doctrine of double predestination, of which Calvin's version is the best-known example. Here, retribution and blessing are not mixed but utterly divided in the claim that by "God's eternal decree . . . eternal life is foreordained for some, eternal damnation for others."[18] The vast majority of Christian believers, among them Calvin's own confessional heirs,[19] have found the doctrine of double predestination to be untenable. No doubt, its distinction between God's eternal election and damnation introduces an inconsistency into the divine life.[20] It is important to see this same inconsistency in the providential explanation. Even though the providential explanation mixes God's comforting will and God's punishing will, this cannot finally hide a double will in God, and so the inconsistency in, and incredibility of, God's causing death.

My proposal rejects any belief in a double will in God. There is a homology, we might say, between the Catholic teaching, embraced by so many other Christian confessions, that God predestines no one to eternal damnation[21] and the claim of my proposal that God does not cause death in any way, in that both positions reject a double will in God and affirm an uncompromising consistency in the divine will toward the creation, sustenance, and fulfillment of life. Whereas much of the tradition has asserted this consistency in the belief that God wills the salvation of all, nearly all Christians have denied this same consistency in the providential explanation's belief that God is benignly at work in the suffering and death God causes. A true consistency in the divine will would set all of God's purposes and actions in opposition to death and refuse to accommodate any divine causality, however comforting, in the workings of suffering and death.

This understanding of God's relationship to death allows innocent suffering to appear fully in a theological account of reality, where its integrity has traditionally been denied. Innocent suffering now can stand as an authentic theological disposition because death no longer marks the universality of human guilt as God's righteous punishment for human sin. If God does not cause death in any way, then the legal explanation's absolute denial of innocent suffering could no longer be maintained. And if the legal explanation's denial of innocent suffering no longer prevails, then the providential explanation's comforting coda to the legal denial is no longer necessary. God's providence can now be detached from the legal explanation so that it stands consistently opposed to suffering and death, and to a suffering and death willed neither retributively nor providentially, in short, to a suffering and death in no way caused by God. A space appears for innocent suffering before the God of life and amidst the suffering and death that besets all created life. That innocent suffering now has a place before God does not mean that human beings are not guilty, and indeed largely guilty, before God. It does mean that human beings suffer innocently, and sometimes scandalously so, before God's own omnipotent providence.

Having come to this theologically constructed space in which innocent suffering abides before a good and all-powerful God, we face all the fundamental issues that gave rise to the legal and providential explanations in the first place. If innocent suffering exists before an omnipotent God, then God's own unlimited power itself would seem to indict God for negligence. The uncompromising guilt that the legal explanation imputes to humanity would shift to God if even a shred of innocent suffering were acknowledged within the broader dimensions of human culpability. My proposal, however, denies any culpability on God's part for suffering and death, since God, on my reading of scripture and tradition, does not cause suffering and death. Yet, even if God does not directly cause suffering and death, God's omnipotence would still seem to make God guilty of indifference toward suffering and death. If God's power toward death is no longer wielded in a causal way, either legally or providentially, then God's unwillingness to end suffering and death, especially innocent suffering and death, would seem to render God guilty. At this point in explanation, a process conception of God would readily renounce the traditional doctrine of divine omnipotence in order to protect God from the charge of culpability. Diminishing God's power while maintaining that God does no evil, as the process conception holds, effectively dispels divine guilt by placing God in the position of paradigmatic innocent sufferer. I am reluctant, however, to turn to a process model of God to address the theological problem of God's relation to evil. The vast majority of Christian believers remain committed to the traditional notion of divine omnipotence and, in that commitment, would find the struggling and limited powers of the process God to be emotionally unsatisfying.

A theological account of God's omnipotence would look to revelation, and not to the logic of a theodicy, to speak effectively of any aspect of the divine life, including God's power. Within the single narrative of scripture and tradition, we can find God's unlimited power revealed in God's scriptural promise to "swallow up death forever" so that "death will be no more" and in the dramatic theory's clear assertion that all the divine energies are aligned against sin, death, and the devil. Revealed omnipotence speaks of a boundless power of God bent on breaking the power of death in all its suffering forms. It is ever engaged in death's destruction as time unfolds from moment to moment. Revealed omnipotence is the power that fulfills God's promise to destroy death in a future that belongs to God. It works to heal the suffering and death of history and accomplishes this healing by the graceful transformation of suffering and death into resurrected life. Revealed omnipotence shows God's power to be diminished in no way whatsoever. It is not an abstract capacity about which reason might speculate but an effective power spoken in a saving promise whose realization can never fail. Finally, revealed omnipotence can be understood in such a way that innocent suffering may enter the field of theological explanation without the unacceptable consequences of God's guiltiness or inability.[22]

Risking Dualism

One last issue needs to be considered. My proposal provides a space for innocent suffering alongside God's saving omnipotence amidst the powers of suffering and death. It does so by removing suffering and death from God's causal agency while affirming God's undiminished omnipotence over suffering and death. Such explanatory moves, though, cannot avoid the age-old question, Whence suffering and death? Certainly we can answer this question to some extent exactly as the classical tradition has. Much suffering and death comes from the human will. Human acts that diminish or destroy the divine gift of life, evil acts, are the cause of a great deal of the suffering and death that continue to ravage history. So much suffering and death, though, issue from causes beyond the human will. The death-dealing power of natural disasters, disease, accident, the impairment of physical and emotional faculties, the debilitation of old age, and the suffering that accompanies so many instances of death itself cannot be understood as volitional outside of a theological frame of reference. Within a traditional theological setting, of course, all these otherwise nonvolitional occasions of suffering and death become thoroughly volitional. According to the legal explanation, human sin causes every suffering and death, even suffering and death apparently beyond human agency that could lie only within God's power. Here God's retribution enacts deathly power that no human will could ever accomplish directly but which is God's only righteous response to the history of human sin. Finally, according to the legal explanation, humanity is responsible for all the suffering and death, for all the evil, of history, even for the suffering and death that only God could do, not as evil but as the just punishment of sin.

Many contemporary theologians who are dissatisfied with the traditional theology of retribution address this problem by regarding death as a natural event and so as an aspect of God's creative plan. Typically, death is understood as an eventuality within the workings of life itself, as a consequence of the opera- tion of the laws of nature that God has created but in which God does not intervene. It is difficult to imagine how reason could interpret death in any way other than as a natural event. A theol- ogy completely committed to reflecting on God in light of a mod- ern scientific worldview would have no choice in regarding death as anything but natural and, to the degree that such a theology still held to a doctrine of creation, in placing death in the divinely willed design for the universe and human life in it. As common as this approach may be as a recent theological option, it is not one that can serve my proposal. The theological claim that death is natural is simply another version of the providential explanation. It places death within the divine will and cannot avoid the theo- logical problem of a double will in God, presuming that the God who wills death into the order of things is still the biblical God who promises to destroy all death.

Once God's causal agency is removed from all death, natural evil in all its manifestations can be interpreted neither as the work of divine justice nor as the work of providential design, whether originally in the primal act of creation or particularly in the cir- cumstances of each person's death. The result of this *theological* denial is that what believers judge to be evil actually increases. An entire contingent of suffering and death that otherwise would be placed under the divine purposes as justice and comfort becomes simply the unadulterated cause of anguish, grief, and loss in human experience. Since this natural evil is not the sort of evil humans could cause, and since, according to my proposal, God does not cause suffering and death, this kind of evil would not be directed by personal agency. It seems to hover in existence as an accompaniment to creation that is not itself created. It appears to be a dimension of evil set in opposition to God's saving energies and that God promises to overwhelm but that courses through history without apparent cause or meaning. In short, my proposal seems to have constructed a dualistic understanding of reality in which a certain kind of evil, caused by no person and inescapably pervasive, has an empty, purposeless, and death-dealing life of its own.

Christianity has always condemned dualism as the most egregious violation of its doctrine of creation, its belief that everything God has created is good and that evil has no real existence in its own right. Classical Christian thought has maintained that evil is a privation, the absence of being and so the absence of the good that everything created possesses. In the history of Christian doctrine, this teaching was formulated in opposition to Gnostic belief, which spoke of evil as a reality, as an evil God who exercised evil power in a material world of this God's making that was itself evil through and through. For the Gnostics, suffering and death have a standing in their own right—a life of their own, so to speak—as acts of the evil God that extend throughout an evil cosmos and that resonate viciously in every physical body. My proposal does not attribute suffering and death to the workings of an evil God. Nor does it maintain that the evil of suffering and death has some metaphysical status in the created order. My configuration of God's relation to evil does not advocate a dualism, the likes of which Christianity has always condemned as irreconcilable with its most basic claims about the character of the creator God.

Admittedly, though, my proposal has risked a dualist position in its willingness to recognize a particular dimension of suffering and death that issues neither from human power nor from divine power and to which God's uncompromising goodness nevertheless is forever opposed. In the context of customary theological assumptions, it is risky to maintain that God has no hand at all in death, not only because such a position seems to limit divine power but also because it recognizes a kind of suffering and death for which there is no personal agency. If there is a kind of suffering and death that has no point of origin in the will of human or divine persons and that is not an aspect of an evilly created world, then this kind of suffering and death would seem to be a self-originating, free-standing power locked in a cosmic battle with the God of life. Even if this kind of suffering and death were not personified, as it typically is in Gnostic mythology, its removal from God's retributive and providential power seems to make it an evil term in a dualism unacceptable to Christian belief.

Once again I must reiterate my rejection of dualism. The free-standing notion of suffering and death presented above need not be regarded as a self-sufficient reality simply because it has no origin in personal agency or in being. As a matter of Christian faith, such suffering and death can be regarded as a privation, as is any evil in the judgment of traditional sensibilities. My proposal only risks a dualism in its insistence that the suffering and death human beings do not do, since they lie beyond their power, are not done by God either. But the risk of dualism, which is finally not dualism at all, is worth the risk in order to allow innocent suffering to enter theological explanation and to describe God's saving work in such a way that removes any hint of a double will in God's relation toward death. Whence, then, the kind of evil that has occupied our attention in this chapter, an evil rampant in the world and for which no personal cause can be assigned? My answer can only be an admission of ignorance.

This, no doubt, is a disappointing response for those expecting a clear solution to the age-old problem of God's relation to evil. It is important to realize, however, that any Christian treatment of this issue will face ignorance in one way or another. Believers meet a wall of ignorance when they question why the God of the legal explanation would bring the punishment of suffering and death on persons who seem so completely innocent. Believers meet a wall of ignorance when they question what purpose the God of the providential explanation might have in willing these or those circumstances of someone's suffering and death. In both instances, ignorance is not merely a response to the unknown. Ignorance becomes a response to the mystery of God's just and loving will, at once retributively and providentially at work in death.

The ignorance we meet in my proposal is not an appropriate response to mystery. An implication of the argument thus far is that much of what the tradition considers to be mysterious about God's relation to death is not mysterious at all, since God does not cause death in any way and since God has revealed God's saving disposition toward death. Upon theological reflection, the only true mystery that remains for believers is why God's promise to destroy death has not been completely fulfilled in the present moment. Our inability to locate the origin of the suffering and death that neither God nor humankind does should not lead us to find mystery in this kind of suffering and death, lest we mystify an evil better regarded simply as a tragic fact of existence. The answer to the questions of where this kind of suffering and death comes from and why its power pervades existence can only be a plea of ignorance. But it is a more productive theological ignorance than one that all too quickly stands unknowing before the supposed mystery of God's agency in death.

The only good reason for risking a dualism in the way we have is to offer a better explanation of God's relation to evil. This chapter has laid out the fundamentals of my proposal as it concerns the issue of divine power. The next chapter continues to examine God's relation to innocent suffering by turning to the doctrine of original sin. Here, we shall build on our discussion thus far by considering God's presence to evil.

Notes

1. Oscar Hijuelos, *Mr. Ives' Christmas* (New York: HarperCollins, 1995), 135.

2. Adela Yarbro Collins, "The Apocalypse (Revelation)," in *The New Jerome Biblical Commentary*, ed. R. E. Brown et al. (Englewood Cliffs, N.J.: Prentice Hall, 1990), 1015.

3. Luther distinguished between "law" and "gospel" in many writings throughout his career. See Gerhard Ebeling, *Luther: An Introduction to His Thought*, trans. R. A. Wilson (Philadelphia: Fortress Press, 1970), 110–24.

4. Ronald F. Thiemann, *Revelation and Theology: The Gospel as Narrated Promise* (Notre Dame, Ind.: University of Notre Dame Press, 1985).

5. Ibid., 112–40. For further reflection on the logic of promise, with special attention to its ethical dimensions, see Margaret A. Farley, *Personal Commitments: Beginning, Keeping, Changing* (San Francisco: Harper & Row, 1986).

6. This most traditional teaching appears even in the same biblical book of Isaiah that has set the exegetical course of my proposal. Later in the text, the speaking God testifies to the extent of God's power over all creation by saying, "I am the Lord, and there is no other. I form light and create darkness, I make weal and create woe; I the Lord do all these things" (Isaiah 45:6–7).

7. Thiemann, *Revelation and Theology*, 109.

8. Gustaf Aulén, *Christus Victor: An Historical Study of the Three Main Types of the Idea of Atonement,* trans. A. G. Herbert (New York: MacMillan, 1969).

9. Ibid., 158.

10. Ibid., 22–28.

11. Ibid., 4.

12. Irenaeus, *Against Heresies* 3.23.1. Quoted in Aulén, *Christus Victor,* 19–20.

13. Athanasius, "On the Incarnation of the Word of God," in *Christology of the Later Fathers,* ed. E. Hardy (Philadelphia: Westminster Press, 1954), 80.

14. Gregory of Nyssa, "Address on Religious Instruction," in *Christology of the Later Fathers,* ed. Hardy, 301.

15. Hannah Arendt, *Eichmann in Jerusalem: A Report on the Banality of Evil* (New York: Viking Press, 1965).

16. Darby Kathleen Ray, *Deceiving the Devil: Atonement, Abuse, and Ransom* (Cleveland, Oh.: Pilgrim Press, 1998), 125–29.

17. Aulén, *Christus Victor,* 14–15, 158.

18. John Calvin, *Institutes of the Christian Religion,* ed. J. T. McNeill (Philadelphia: Westminster Press, 1977), 2:926.

19. "The concept which so hampered the traditional doctrine [of double predestination] was that of an equilibrium or balance in which blessedness was ordained and declared on the right hand [of God] and perdition on the left. This concept we must oppose with all the emphasis of which we are capable" (Karl Barth, *Church Dogmatics,* vol. II, 2, trans. G. W. Bromiley et al. [Edinburgh: T. & T. Clark, 1957], 171).

20. One finds equally clear representations of a double will in God in some stances in post-Holocaust Judaism. A good example is David Blumenthal, who has argued that the God of the covenant is best understood as an abusive parent in relation to the Jewish people. God, for Blumenthal, is abusive in God's actions toward Israel, though not always. Blumenthal develops this position in order to explain the problem of innocent suffering. His deeply unsatisfactory proposal is actually quite typical in its positing a double will in God, however shocking the clarity of the double will may be in Blumenthal's account. See David Blumenthal, *Facing the Abusing God: A Theology of Protest* (Louisville, Ky.: Westminster/John Knox Press, 1993), esp. 237–48.

21. Henricus Denzinger-Adolfus Schönmetzer, *Enchiridion Symbolorum Definitionem et Declarationem de Rebus Fidei et Morum,* 34th ed. (Freiburg im Breisgau: Herder, 1967), 137, no. 397.

22. I agree with Marilyn McCord Adams's general claim that the very character of the biblical God is oriented toward the defeat of horrendous evil but disagree with her accompanying claim that this divine

action must be accomplishable within an individual person's life and in a sufficient enough way so that the victim judges his or her life to be worth living. It seems to me that this expectation fails to imagine the extent of the truly horrendous and makes personal judgment the validation of God's power over evil. Adams seems to require a historical criterion for judging the possibility of meaning in suffering, a good indication that her proposal, with all its appeal to the biblical tradition, is finally committed to a logical explanation, however different from the many theodicies she criticizes. See Marilyn McCord Adams, *Horrendous Evils and the Goodness of God* (Ithaca, N.Y.: Cornell University Press, 1999).

∴ 4 ∴

Beyond Retribution

INNOCENT SUFFERING
IN A FALLEN WORLD

IT SEEMS STRANGE to say that God does not cause suffering and death in any way, and to say so in the name of traditional theological sensibilities. This is an idea foreign to the classical tradition, which insists on God's absolute causal power, wielded even in the terrible power of death. Recently, process theologians have been willing to deny God's causality in death, but only as an expression of a more general and untraditional theological position that diminishes divine ability, not only God's agency in death but also God's saving power. Many believers who are offended by the providential explanation, while otherwise pleased to have God's causal power distanced from death, would be reluctant to pay the high price exacted by the process understanding of God. God's omnipotence, particularly as exercised in God's consummate defeat of death, is the basis for the faith that many believers place in the divine person. My proposal voices this emotional expectation that believers have of the living God who saves. God, I have argued, has no causal role to play in death, and claiming as much need not come at the cost of God's absolute providential power. God, I have maintained, is utterly powerful over death through a revealed omnipotence that transforms suffering and death into the glory of eternal life. Granted, the denial of God's causal agency in death seems strange to traditional sensibilities. Yet I have argued for such a position within the broader assumptions of Christian belief in order to make room for innocent suffering in an otherwise traditional Christian worldview.

My discussion in the preceding chapter tried to establish the theological integrity of innocent suffering by addressing the issue of God's power. Denying God's causal agency in death subverted the legal explanation's claim that suffering and death in every life are the work of God's retributive justice, God's righteous response to the inescapability of human guilt. Taking innocent suffering seriously, as my proposal does, does not entail a denial of human guilt, as though innocence and guilt are mutually exclusive. Guilt pervades every life and all of history as a response to the evil acts that human beings commit. My argument thus far has negotiated the doctrinal tradition by making a single modification in its many interrelated teachings: that human guilt does not completely eclipse human innocence in suffering. This one change in customary assumptions has had far-reaching consequences. It led us to reconceive God's relation to evil by setting God utterly at odds with suffering and death, and not at all behind them as intending cause. This understanding of divine power released the providential explanation from its ties to the legal explanation and collapsed God's double will into a single, consistent, and comforting disposition on God's part toward death. Now we must consider the consequences of this same single modification for the traditional doctrine of original sin.

The doctrine of original sin—that all humanity is born into a state of sin and so stands guilty before God—seems to be directly incompatible with any claim for the integrity of innocent suffering. If innocent suffering exists at all, then the doctrine of original sin, it would seem, is not a truthful representation of the human condition before God. Furthermore, making space for the integrity of innocent suffering before God results in a particular understanding of divine power, one that denies God's agency in death. This agency, however, is exactly what the doctrine of original sin affirms. God brings about suffering and death as humanity's deserved punishment for the sin of Adam and its continued reenactment in every life. According to the traditional doctrine,

God's intention in causing death is neither capricious nor satisfying. It is God's just response to the undeniable guilt of humanity.
The legal explanation ties God's agency in death to original sin.
Denying God's agency in this regard, as I have, seems to deny the
doctrine of original sin as well, since the presence of such sin traditionally requires God's retributive punishment in causing
death, if God is to be just.

In this chapter, I shall argue that there is an understanding of
original sin that is compatible with the two premises in our proposal thus far—that innocent suffering exists and that God has no
agency at all in death. The challenge in framing such an understanding is that it must, in principle, be different from the formulation of the doctrine that has endured for so long in Christian
belief. To many, the simple fact of difference is necessarily the
proof of deviation. Yet compatibility never is a matter of repeti-
tion but instead a matter of congruence among the tradition's
broader assumptions and novel theological claims. The development of tradition through history sometimes moves by the repe-
tition of beliefs from generation to generation. Often, however,
tradition develops more malleably as the basic claims of faith are
experienced anew, and so somewhat differently, in each historical
moment. Congruence between and among past and present
claims of faith is the first ingredient in shaping the continuity
across the ages that believers call "tradition."[1] Congruence,
though, is a relation that presumes difference within the congru-
ent positions. A claim for theological congruence needs to show
how a real continuity with the faith of the past abides among the
differences that usually arise when believers express their faith in
any present moment. My understanding of original sin aims at
such congruence.

Most treatments of the doctrine of original sin find their
place in systematic theology under the heading of "theological
anthropology," since they explain the condition of the human
person before God. Typically, theological anthropologies that are
conservative in orientation stress humanity's sinful alienation
from God and the utter gratuity of grace.[2] Theological anthropologies that are liberal in orientation find a deep attraction to
God in human nature that strives for graceful meaning, even in

the midst of the sinfulness that prevents this inclination from reaching satisfaction.[3] Even though the exposition of original sin can move in these somewhat different directions, both approaches try to give theological account of the tragic dimensions of human existence. My approach will not neglect the typically anthropological concerns of the doctrine of original sin in its theological development, though it will depart from traditional treatments in its particular attention to God's relation to original sin. God, of course, has a role to play in the traditional account of original sin. God is the judge who wields the power of retribution, the divine verdict of death for all. My interest in God's place in the doctrine of original sin has a different point of departure. If our concern is to show how the doctrine of original sin can be articulated in a way that yet acknowledges the reality of innocent suffering, then a significant part of that task will involve explaining how God's goodness remains credible before the moral fact of such suffering.

Whereas the previous chapter developed a theology of innocent suffering by focusing on God's power, this chapter is concerned with God's presence. The Christian tradition believes in God's oneness, and in that oneness God's power and presence must finally be the same. There is, however, a long history of theological reflection on the divine attributes, the distinguishable traits of God's one divine being that manifest how God is God in being and in action. My particular attention here to the divine attribute of omnipresence will enable us to appreciate further how God is disposed toward human beings in sin who are yet, at times, beleaguered innocently by suffering and death. I shall proceed by sifting through the assumptions of the traditional doctrine of original sin for a conception of the pervasiveness of human guilt compatible with the untraditional theological premise that people do suffer innocently.

A Short History of Sin:
Paul, Augustine, and the Council of Trent

The doctrine of original sin does not appear among the beliefs of the earliest Christians. There is no mention of original sin in the

New Testament, nor is there any conceptualization in its pages that matches what was to become, centuries later, the church's accepted doctrine of original sin. Like most of the fundamental teachings of the Christian tradition, the church's orthodox belief about original sin developed in the course of time and took a definitive step toward its present shape in a tumultuous setting of disagreement about what the church's true faith should be. Augustine's theological battles with the Pelagians in the early fifth century on the role of divine grace in salvation provided a controversial context for the development of the doctrine of original sin. Although one can find hints of Augustine's stance in earlier Christian writers, there is a real sense in which Augustine is the author of this enduring Christian teaching.

Yet the strong notion of sin formalized in the traditional doctrine through Augustine's theology does have an important precedent in the writings of Paul. As I have noted earlier, Paul's understanding of human sinfulness does not exhibit all the features of the later doctrine of original sin, particularly its claim that human sinfulness is inherited by birth. Paul, though, does say that sin is inescapable, a theological premise that lies at the heart of the later doctrine of original sin. He regards this inescapable quality of sin as an evil, irresistible imitation that he explains through a certain reading of the Genesis story. Adam, Paul states, is the originator of sin and, in Paul's remarkable interpretation of the ancient Hebrew text, the originator of death as well:

> Therefore, just as sin came into the world through one man, and death came through sin, and so death spread to all because all have sinned—sin was indeed in the world before the law, but sin is not reckoned when there is no law. Yet death exercised dominion from Adam to Moses, even over those whose sins were not like the transgression of Adam. . . . (Romans 5:12–14)

In Paul's reading of Genesis, Adam's sin causes death, and the proof of sin's utter pervasiveness is that all human beings die. The spread of sin, in Paul's thinking, seems to lie not in its presence from birth but instead in the bad example of the first parents, whose rebellion against God is tragically repeated in every human life. Irresistible imitation, not birth, is the source of the sin that arises in every human life and by which, Paul claims, all are enslaved (Romans 7:14).

Paul's causal linking of death to sin derives from his interpretation of the consequences of sin in the Genesis story. God pronounces punishment on Adam and Eve for embracing the serpent's temptation that they, in spite of their creatureliness, could actually "be like God" (Genesis 3:5). These punishments, like God's creation of the world, become reality by virtue of their being spoken by God. In gender stereotypical fashion, the text identifies God's punishment of Eve and all her daughters with "the pain [with which women] shall bring forth children," and perhaps also with the subjugation of the wife to her husband (Genesis 3:16). Drawing on gender stereotype again, the text has God's punishment of Adam and all his sons issue "in toil," in the difficulties of labor in tilling the land for sustenance (Genesis 3:16). In the last of the punishing pronouncements, God says to Adam, "By the sweat of your face you shall eat bread until you return to the ground, for out of it you were taken; you are dust and to dust you shall return" (Genesis 3:19).

Perhaps the most literal way to read this last punishment would be as a further description of the hardships, specifically those that will vex men as a result of sin. Cultivating the land for food will be an onerous, lifelong task, ending only with death and "return to the ground." The concluding words of the passage— "you are dust and to dust you shall return"—could be read in this context simply as an observation of fact, offered here as an expression of divine amazement at the arrogance of sinful intention. Adam and, through him, Eve were formed "from the dust of the ground" in the second creation story in Genesis (2:7). Read as an observation of fact, the divine words describe the creaturely limitations God chose even for the most exalted of all creatures. Human existence has a beginning, unlike God's existence, and it has an end, unlike God's existence. Given these limitations, God's words convey a sense of tragic astonishment that Adam, in all his creatureliness, could ever have imagined that he could be like God and through such an evil aspiration subvert God's gift of relationship to humanity. Paul, however, does not read Genesis 3:19 in this way. For Paul, the words "you are dust and to dust you shall return" are not a divine observation of created fact but a curse, the moment at which God brought death into the created order as a punishment for the first sin. In Paul's reading, sin causes death since sin prompts God's only righteous response to human treachery, a punishment that extends from the first parents to all their descendants.

This early Christian reading rests on an important assumption. If death is divine punishment for sin, then human beings presumably were created immortal by God and lost the state of immortality through sin and God's retribution. Had Adam and Eve not sinned and had they not provided the terribly compelling example that all their children imitate, death would never have entered history. Death, in such a reading, was not part of God's original plan for the created order. Through Paul's tremendous influence, Christians have come to assume that the first sin brought God's retribution in death, which subverted humanity's created immortality. This is not, however, the only understanding of death in the earlier Jewish tradition. The author of Sirach, for example, expresses the view of some Jewish interpreters, ancient and rabbinic, that death is not a divine punishment but God's willed end to human life, the way in which God chose to create beings in God's own image and likeness (Sirach 41:1–4).[4] Paul's reading was not unprecedented in the earlier Jewish tradition, and it continued to be made in the later rabbinic tradition. What made it unique was the authoritative role it came to play in the developing Christian tradition. There are several reasons for its influence.

First, Paul's reading provided an existential proof for the universality of sin in everyone's death, an important message for Christianity's first-century mission to the Gentile world. In order to preach the gospel to the Gentiles, Paul had to modify the background beliefs of the earliest Jewish Christians, particularly their traditional notion of suffering as exile, the loss of God's promised land as divine punishment for breaking the covenant. Exile was the particular and actual historical experience of the Jewish people. Exile, to say nothing of exile endowed with religious meaning, is not the experience of all peoples. Paul's reinterpretation of Genesis thus enabled his non-Jewish audience to name a universal corruption in their own lives healed by the gospel's message of universal grace. Second, Paul's insistence on the inescapability of sin denied innocent suffering and by doing so protected God from the guilt that only sinful humanity deserved. Third, as Elaine Pagels has noted, the oddly attractive side of Paul's claim that death marks the universality of guilt is that it makes every sinful person an actor in the drama of salvation.[5] As terrible as this guilt is, its just suffering brings a legal symmetry to life preferable to helplessness. It helps (some, at least) to believe that suffering is deserved. Fourth, and finally, Paul's strong view of sin seems compellingly true, not only for the psychological reason that Pagels identifies but also as a description of a world in which sin and death are pervasive. There certainly are ways to portray the universality of sin other than by linking sin to death as punishment. However the universality of sin is represented symbolically, the claim that an evil of human making saturates the world resonates with the experience of virtually everyone.

The New Testament assumes that God's salvation breaks the hold of sin and death over life. But of all the depictions of sin in the New Testament—as demonic possession, as the evil powers that control the universe, as disease, as the anti-Christ, as moral weakness and betrayal—none receives more explicit explanation than Paul's influential reading of the Genesis story in Romans 5. Paul's reading may not yet be a doctrine of original sin as it was later defined. It provided, though, the crucial themes on which Augustine offered variations that took shape as the tradition's accepted doctrine.

Augustine's change of mind from conversion to later career is a tale often told in narrating the history of Christian thought. The *Confessions*, a spiritual autobiography that Augustine wrote in mid-career around the year 400, tells the story of its author's early life to his conversion in the year 386. This account, written some fourteen years after its central event, presents a story of the irresistibility of divine grace through which God, in pursuit of the young Augustine throughout his life, demolished the convert's sinful resistance to God's saving will. Readers of the *Confessions* can easily see a Pauline plot in its pages. As much as sin abounded in Augustine's life, God's grace came to abound all the more. As much as Augustine's will was enslaved by the deathly power of sin before which free choice was powerless, God's will brought the freedom of faith and the undeserved inheritance of eternal life. Careful attention to the writings Augustine penned immediately after his conversion, however, tell a different story. Many of these controversial writings against the Manicheans, such as *On Free Choice of the Will*, portray sin as the result of an evil choice that could have been made otherwise. For the early Augustine, sin abounds, but not irresistibly so. Just as the will may turn by choice to lesser goods as though they were the highest good and by doing so fall into sin, the will may also choose to follow the divine law, God's own will, and by doing so practice virtue. The young Augustine has such confidence in human moral capacity that he describes human reason as naturally oriented to God's law and as the will's guide in every virtuous act.[6] By the time he wrote the *Confessions*, Augustine had changed his mind considerably about the will's power over moral choice, and this provided a context for the development of the traditional doctrine of original sin.

Augustine tells several stories in the *Confessions* that anticipate his anti-Pelagian position on the depths of human sin. In the jealousy of one baby for another being breast-fed in its place, Augustine sees the power of evil and the absence of innocence even in those too young to choose responsibly.[7] A boyhood prank of stealing pears from a neighbor's orchard for no purpose but the fruit's wanton destruction illustrates the "greedy love of doing wrong" for its own sake.[8] Augustine tells the story of his good friend Alypius, who as a young man was so addicted to the blood-sport of the gladiatorial games that he could not make his eyes stop watching the spectacles by which his mind was repulsed.[9] And from beginning to end, Augustine presents his life story up to his conversion as a single act of sinful resistance to God's loving will. If we find Augustine's understanding of original sin narrated in the plot of his personal story, we find it explained as orthodox Christian doctrine in his writings against the Pelagians.

Pelagius and his disciples, such as Coelestius and Julian of Eclanum, were Augustine's literary opponents in a battle for Christian truth that lasted for the last twenty years of his life. Pelagius's teaching made a heroic asceticism the model of true

Christian discipleship and the goal of every believer. In his letter to Demetrias, a young woman contemplating entry to the religious life, Pelagius gives advice for Christian living that sets a high moral standard for the follower of Christ:

> A power that is to be exercised must therefore be brought out into full attention, and the good of which nature is capable must be clearly explained. Once something has been shown possible, it ought to be accomplished. . . . Showing a person that he can actually achieve what he desires provides the most effective incentives for the soul. Even in warfare, the best way to influence and encourage a soldier is to remind him of his own power.[10]

Augustine was quick to see that this religious understanding of human nature made too little of God's grace and too much of human initiative in the attainment of eternal life. Pelagius expected much from the human will because he believed that God had endowed it with a moral strength that Adam's primal sin had not significantly damaged. In Augustine's judgment, this moral optimism simply did not fit with the evidence of every human life or with the evidence of history. To make too little of God's grace and too much of human initiative was to make too little of sin and the extent to which every person stood in need before God. This, for Augustine, was Pelagius's heretical error.

All of Augustine's anti-Pelagian writings—from *On the Spirit and the Letter* (412) to his incomplete work *Against Julian,* still in preparation at the time of his death in 430—give every bit of credit to God in the work of salvation. God's grace, and no noble human initiative at all, brings humanity to resurrected life. In these works, Augustine leaves behind the position he advocated in *On Free Choice of the Will.* Whereas that early writing portrayed the will as empowered to choose good or evil, the path to God or the path to perdition, the anti-Pelagian tracts gradually present free choice in a distinctly Pauline fashion, as a power that can only choose to sin in spite of its ability to recognize the moral good. Augustine roots this incapacity of the will for a real, effective choice between good and evil in the effects of Adam's sin. Much like Paul, Augustine conceives of the first sin as a rupture in the relationship between humanity and God that reverberates in every human life. Augustine, however, does not depict the force of the primal sin as irresistible imitation. Instead, he situates sin in the human nature every person brings into the world, thus making the power of sin its inherence in the metaphysical constitution of every self. Augustine would agree with Paul that all human beings imitate the sin of the first parents, and do so irresistibly. The inescapability of sin for Augustine lies finally, though, in the sin with which all are born as an evil inheritance that is actualized in every irresistible act of sinning. Pelagius and his followers refused to acknowledge this sin that precedes sinning, and by this error they made God's grace unnecessary, as though humanity by its own power could achieve eternal life. "The fault of our nature," Augustine insists, "remains in our offspring so deeply impressed as to make it guilty, even when the guilt of the self-same fault has been washed away in the parent by the remission of sins—until every defect which ends in sin by the consent of the human will is consumed and done away in the last regeneration [the future resurrection]."[11]

Like Paul, Augustine understands the primal sin in every life as the legal consequence of Adam's fall. He maintains that sin causes God's righteous punishment of death and that the universality of sin and death is the measure of human need before God's grace. Augustine, though, goes further than Paul by including sexual desire in the mix of human experience that demonstrates the universality of sin. The desire for self-indulgence, especially in sexual desire, marks the effective power of original sin in every life. Sexual desire becomes, in Augustine's theological analysis, a measure of human powerlessness before the sin whose manifestation it is. Whereas the young Augustine expected much of reason and will in moral practice, the older Augustine of the Pelagian controversy found them to be vanquished by the passion that, he believed, coursed through every human life as a symptom of sin's deep-seated pathology. "This lust," Augustine states in chapter 14 of *City of God*,

> assumes power not only over the whole body, and not only from the outside, but also internally; it disturbs the whole man, when the mental emotion combines and mingles with the physical craving, resulting in a pleasure surpassing all physical delights.

> So intense is the pleasure that when it reaches its climax there is
> an almost total extinction of mental alertness; the intellectual
> sentries as it were, are overwhelmed. Now surely any friend of
> wisdom and holy joys who leads a married life . . . would prefer,
> if possible, to beget children without lust of this kind.[12]

The irresistible power of death has an analogue in the irresistible
power of sexual lust and its physical pleasure. Lust overwhelms
the body, causing the genitals to defy reason and will if not in the
consummation of desire then in the welling up of passion itself.
The powerlessness of the person before death and desire manifests the guilty powerlessness of the person before the sin into
which all humanity is born.

We have already seen that Paul's understanding of death as
punishment for Adam's sin assumes that death does not exist
prior to sin and that human beings are created immortal. Augustine shares Paul's assumption and argues in a parallel fashion for
a state of human existence before the primal sin in which the evil
of sexual desire had not yet come to be. Just as death has an analogue in sexual desire, prelapsarian immortality has an analogue
in prelapsarian passionlessness. Marriage and procreation
through sexual intercourse, Augustine insists, existed prior to the
first sin. They were ordained by God as part of the created plan
and so are good. Had the first parents not sinned, the lust that
now tragically accompanies sexual intercourse would never have
made its appearance in the sexual act, reserved in paradise for the
procreation of children in marriage. Had paradise lasted, Augustine speculates, "the parts created for this task would be the servants of [the] mind, even in their function of procreation . . . [and]
begin their activity at the bidding of the will, instead of being
stirred up by the ferment of lust."[13] Whereas Paul marked the universality of sin by the death of all that sin causes, Augustine adds
to this ultimate marker an original one, fixed in life's beginnings
and appearing in the body's constant, fallen desires. Although he
never made up his mind on the matter, Augustine was inclined in
his later writings to understand the origin of every person's soul
in the act of procreation.[14] This view, known as traducianism, was
attractive to Augustine because it enabled him to regard the origin of every person as spoiled by the inheritance of Adam's sin

passed down from parents to child in the biological act of repro-
duction. Original sin, in this explanation, is communicated in the
very act of lustful sexual intercourse that itself marks Adam's dis-
obedience to God on every body.

Death and sexual desire, pain and pleasure, life's end and
life's beginning all become the manifestation of original sin's universality in Augustine's explanation, a position that extends
Paul's account of the terrible consequences of sin even further
into the existential circumstances of life.[15] Augustine's delin-
eation of the doctrine of original sin, of course, could not make
theological sense apart from the very strong doctrine of grace
that Augustine also developed in the course of the Pelagian controversy. Original sin may subvert every human power that might
be applied to the attainment of eternal happiness. God's love,
though, breaks the power of this sin that precedes sinning and all
its lustful and deathly effects. In Augustine's estimation, God's
grace is not offered since it could not be chosen or even received
by an act of the human will. All humanity stands under God's
decree of divine punishment on Adam, a decree issued again and
again in the original sin into which all are born. God, however,
has pronounced another, eternal decree to bestow resurrected life
on those whom God has chosen to share a heavenly inheritance.
Those timelessly predestined by God's saving choice are rescued
from the perdition that original sin would bring to all, were it not
for this inscrutable act of the divine will that imputes sainthood
to those utterly undeserving of such honor.[16] As the kind of theologian who attributes all saving glory to God and all damning
guilt to humanity, Augustine follows the logic of such religious
sensibilities to their only conclusion by advocating a strong doctrine of predestination.

As intertwined as the doctrines of original sin and predestination are in Augustine's later thought, much of the later Christian tradition regarded them as distinct. Many of the Protestant
reformers of the sixteenth century—Luther, Zwingli, and Calvin
among them—followed Augustine's lead by marrying a strong
understanding of original sin to a strong understanding of God's
predestinating grace. The Catholic tradition, however, has never
been comfortable with the partnership of sin and grace in Augus-

tine's later thought, despite Augustine's undisputed authority throughout the medieval period. The Second Council of Orange (529) upheld Augustine's teaching on original sin while condemning the notion of double predestination, the view that God eternally wills the salvation of some and eternally wills the damnation of others.[17] Although Augustine had never argued in any protracted way for double predestination, some of his statements in the anti-Pelagian writings were certainly susceptible to such an interpretation.[18] The Council of Trent (1545–1563) condemned several teachings of the Protestant reformers on sin and grace that they themselves supported by appeal to the later Augustine. Trent's "Decree on Justification" (1547) reiterated Orange's rejection of double predestination, but qualified its strong emphasis on human corruption by rejecting any understanding of original sin that made humanity utterly powerless before God's grace. According to Trent, humanity stands under Adam's fault as "slaves of sin . . . and under the power of the devil and of death." Yet the same humanity, though under the sway of original sin, still possesses a free will that, "though weakened and unsteady, was by no means destroyed."[19]

The Council of Trent negotiated the Augustinian tradition in other ways that highlight the diversity of Christian positions on original sin. Augustine's regard for sexual desire as a bodily mark of original sin suggested that concupiscent desire was itself sin, a position explicitly advocated by Luther and Calvin. In Trent's teaching, inordinate desire is a temptation that may lead to sin if human free choice succumbs to its seductive power. This temptation, though, can and should be overcome by the free will, integrity, and responsibility that still dwell in human nature after the Fall in Catholic teaching. The Council of Trent nonetheless affirmed many features of the tradition's Augustinian legacy on original sin, particularly in its claims that Adam's sin "is communicated to all . . . by propagation not by imitation" and in such a way that through original sin all persons have "incurred the death" by which God brings punishment to humanity.[20] Trent clearly acknowledges the sin that precedes sinning so distasteful to Augustine's Pelagian opponents and in its teaching stands squarely within the assumptions of the traditional legal explanation.

Adam's Fault, Universalized

There is, then, a diversity of theological and confessional views on original sin and the religious understanding of human nature before God that it implies. And yet, amidst this diversity, a consistency abides in the most basic beliefs that all representations of original sin convey. However sin is lodged in human nature—as irresistible imitation or as the inheritance of conception and birth—and however the consequences of sin are conceived—as pain, as enervating labor of all sorts, as death, or as lust—and however the capacity of the human will is portrayed in the face of this fallenness—as powerless and passive or as able to some degree and responsible—all representations of original sin that we find in the tradition describe sinfulness as universal. This representation conveys the Christian experience of the inescapability of sin, and so too faith's appreciation for the deep need in which human beings stand before God's saving grace. The universality of sin means that all human beings without exception are guilty before God's righteousness and that grace enters every human life therefore as an unmerited gift, as God's surprising response to the pervasiveness of human guilt.

This consistent teaching on the universality of sin and guilt has typically been conceived in a way that makes innocent suffering impossible in a Christian worldview. Guilt's universality is imagined to be so utterly complete that innocent suffering evaporates without remainder. The teaching of Trent, we should note, does acknowledge a postlapsarian state of innocence enjoyed by those who have just been baptized and who have not yet entered into the history of personal sin that itself is one of the terrible consequences of the Fall. In opposition to any view of human nature utterly ravaged by Adam's sin, the council taught that "through the grace of our Lord Jesus Christ conferred in baptism the guilt of original sin is . . . remitted" and that those who have been regenerated by baptism "are made innocent, without stain, pure, no longer hateful, but beloved sons of God, heirs, indeed of God and joint heirs with Christ."[21] Yet this extraordinary state of innocence is a kind of theological abstraction that intended primarily to affirm the efficacy of baptism and the Catholic belief in the baptized person's real responsibility to, and free choice before, God. This innocence lasts only as long as the baptized person remains free of sin, and so is divorced from the existential circumstances of life in which, according to Catholic belief, free choice is exercised and inevitably fails.

In any case, this state of innocence after the guilt of original sin and prior to personal sin does not extend to innocent *suffering*, since suffering and death remain God's retribution for the sin of Adam that, in traditional Christian teaching, all justly deserve. Considered existentially, in the history of sin's consequences, guilt remains as universal as the death it brings and banishes innocent suffering from the viable assumptions of Christian belief. In spite of their differences, then, the Catholic and Protestant traditions are both deeply committed to the thick universality of sin and guilt in the Augustinian heritage, a conception of universality that effectively denies the theological possibility of innocent suffering.

It should not surprise us that a universality so thick would be symbolized as palpable and concrete. Through Augustine, the tradition has come to see the universality of sin and guilt both in death and in sexual desire, the body's undeniable proofs of the will's powerlessness in the tragic history of sin. These existential markers of sin's universality have also come to be linked to God's punishment of sin. For Augustine, the universality of death and lust are twin symptoms of the guilt all possess in sin, as well as divine retribution for the treachery against God that all persons enter life ready to do. There is a sense in which Augustine's famous introspective testimony in the *Confessions* to God's intimate presence—"You were more inward than my inmost self"[22]— could be paraphrased to describe the understanding of sin that Augustine bequeathed to the tradition: sin is more inward than our inmost, fallen self. Sin is as inward as the desire and death that riddle every human body as guilty forms of retributive suffering. In the Augustinian tradition, innocent suffering is as impossible as the absence of desire or the ability to will oneself never to die, for both the pleasure of sexual desire and the inevitability of death are divinely willed punishments, universal sentences that redress the universality of sin and guilt.

It is not difficult to understand why death and divine punishment would be linked in the development of the traditional doctrine of original sin. Punishment entails suffering, and death
often enters life attended by physical and emotional suffering,
whether the death one faces is one's own or, as it more frequently
is, the death of a friend or loved one. It is far more difficult to see
how sexual desire and sexual pleasure could be regarded as God's
punishing response to the primal sin. Augustine may find it obvious that sexual pleasure is a deeply troubling, disorienting, and
finally painful experience that metes out divine punishment, as
he testifies in the passage from chapter 14 of *City of God* quoted
earlier. But few would agree with his judgment and far fewer
would consider it obvious! As any number of recent commentators have noted, Augustine's identification of sexual pleasure, sin,
and divine punishment voices the day-to-day struggles of an
ascetic whose commitment to celibacy encourages him to define
temptation and the ravages of sin in terms of bodily pleasure. The
authority of this ascetical paradigm in Christian history has
enabled Augustine's ascetical experience—in fact the experience
of relatively few—to become encoded in Christian values as the
experience of all and, along with death, as one of original sin's
bodily markers.

One of the achievements of contemporary theology has been
to show that this ascetical approach to Christian discipleship is
one among others and need not set a standard before which non-
ascetical forms of Christian practice are necessarily judged inferior. Elizabeth Dreyer, for example, has argued for an "everyday"
spirituality that seeks God in the lives of laypeople—in their work,
in their friendships, in their parenting, and even, *pace Augustine*,
in their love-making. Sexual passion, like anything created, may
be a medium of sinfulness. But it also, Dreyer recognizes, may be
a sacramental encounter with God's infinite love that, in its physicality, reflects God's own embrace of physicality in the incarnation. Dreyer suggests too that the attraction consummated in the
physical union of persons in love expresses the same yearning for
union with God articulated in the writings of the great mystics.[23]

Sexual desire and original sin are so interwoven in the Augustinian tradition that Dreyer's ideas could only seem subversive to

someone deeply immersed in that tradition's assumptions. Yet Dreyer's willingness to find theological value in sexual desire and pleasure does not lead her to deny the most basic claims of the classical doctrine of original sin. Her proposal for an "everyday" spirituality affirms the fallenness of humanity and human nature's inability to merit the grace that God bestows as an undeserved gift.

Dreyer is not concerned directly with the doctrine of original sin. Her efforts to find theological meaning in bodiliness, however, lead her to criticize the Augustinian understanding of the doctrine indirectly. In order to overcome the Augustinian conflation of sin and sexual desire, Dreyer implicitly distinguishes between the most basic features of the doctrine, namely, the universality of sin and the gratuity of grace, and a particular way of communicating those features that has been tremendously influential in the tradition, and yet need not be. Between the lines of her theological proposal, Dreyer points to ways in which the doctrine of original sin might be constructed so that the traditional linkage of sin and sexuality is broken while the profound truth of the traditional doctrine remains intact in another faithful configuration of the doctrine.

We can learn from Dreyer's strategy as we continue to consider God's relationship to evil. Our concern, though, is not with the traditional identification of sin and sexual desire but with the traditional identification of sin and death that is characteristic of the Pauline-Augustinian heritage. Our reconstructive task with respect to the second bodily marker for the universality of original sin is much more difficult. As we have seen, there is something counterintuitive about regarding sexual desire and pleasure as divine punishment. Only the remarkable authority accorded to ascetical discipleship in Christian history could account for such an explanation. Exposing the hegemony of the ascetical paradigm in Christian spirituality, as Dreyer does so well, allows one to see what is rather obvious to those standing outside an Augustinian circle of explanation—that bodily pleasure is not suffering that delivers God's punishment. But since death brings physical and emotional suffering to the lives it enters, the Pauline-Augustinian connection between death and divine punishment is not

counterintuitive at all. The Christian imagination has readily
seized upon death in all its suffering forms as a powerful way to
align a universal and just divine punishment with the universality
of guilt. In many respects, it is the uncompromising universality
of death and deathliness that stands behind the tradition's consistent denial of innocent suffering. The traditional understanding of divine omnipotence, which expects God to be the causal
agent of death, only bolsters this connection between the universality of guilt and the universality of death.

The preceding chapter argued that God is not the cause of
death in order to make space for innocent suffering in a Christian
worldview. This position amounted to a refutation of the legal
explanation, which, in the setting of Christian assumptions,
aligns death as divine punishment to the utterly universal guilt of
fallen humanity. Since what I have called the legal explanation *is*
the traditional doctrine of original sin, it may seem that the argument developed thus far could only entail the denial of the traditional doctrine. If God does not do death in any way, and if God,
as a consequence, does not bring death into life as a just punishment for the universality of human guilt, then it follows that
humanity is not universally guilty before God and perhaps even
not guilty at all. Dreyer's analysis, however, has shown how at least
one bodily marker for the universality of human guilt can be dis-
connected from the claims of the traditional doctrine without a
loss to the doctrine's integrity. My task in the remainder of the
chapter is to show how the most basic claims of the traditional
doctrine can be affirmed even as the bodily marker of death is
uncoupled from the universality of guilt, which any adequate
account of original sin must maintain. My explanation ventures
more. I shall argue that the denial of God's causality in death and
the affirmation of innocent suffering that emerges in the space of
this denial enable us to appreciate both the depths of human sin
and God's presence to those who suffer innocently.

Innocent Suffering in the Midst of Guilty Suffering

A faithful reconstruction of the doctrine of original sin would follow the classical representation in most respects. Above all, a

faithful account would affirm the power of a sin that precedes sinning. Contemporary Christians, no doubt, would be more inclined toward a functionalist understanding of this tragic precedence of sin. Such an understanding of sin explains human fallenness by focusing on how human behavior actually "functions" in committing evil acts. A functionalist understanding of sin is closer to Paul's understanding than to Augustine's and speaks of human fallenness as an inheritance that all bring into the world by virtue of the evil that all humanity has done and to which every human being will tragically contribute. This functionalist view does not make original sin a matter of biological inheritance, as the traducianist explanation does. Modern biology has made remarkable advances in documenting the role that genetics plays in shaping the vital constitution of every person, and there is little likelihood that the Human Genome Project will turn up a genetic basis for original sin. The traducianist view is problematic not only in light of modern biology but also with regard to the support it lends to the Augustinian identification of sin and sexual passion. The criticism of theologians like Elizabeth Dreyer has made it difficult, if not impossible, for ascetical assumptions to configure the tradition's symbolism of belief in an exclusive way.

A functionalist view of original sin would understand the precedence of sin from the perspective of the sinning that every individual does in life as an act of defiance toward the goodness that God eternally has willed for the created order. This promulgation of evil by discrete acts of the will creates a social dimension to sin into which all are born. According to Christian belief, no individual can transcend this sin that precedes sinning. Its givenness does not coerce the will in a way that violates the human capacity for free choice affirmed so strongly by the Council of Trent. The sin that precedes acts of sinning in any individual life does not subvert the real acts of virtue that may be accomplished in any particular instance. Precedent sin, whether one's own or the collective sin of the entire human race, can be resisted in any moment of moral choice. But a functionalist view of original sin faithful to tradition would insist that the social inheritance of sin does have a determinative and tragic influence on every individual born. Although it would be fashionable in our culture to conceive of this tragic influence only in terms of the ways persons are victimized by their lot in life—by the state of health, by the family, by the socioeconomic circumstances into which they are born—this approach would not adequately convey what the tradition means by original sin. Precedent sin does have a victimizing power. Its most terrible truth, however, is that all persons in the course of their lives will become victimizers, whether through their own aggressive actions or through their indirect, though very real, participation in victimizing social forces.

Contemporary theology has offered productive ways to conceive of the kind of precedent sin that we encounter as victims. Latin American liberation theologians such as Gustavo Gutiérrez call attention to the ways an economic system like free market capitalism creates an enslaving bondage of poverty for so many people in the Third World.[24] As a coda to Gutiérrez's critique we should note that the same economic system, itself the result of daily acts of the human will, also creates a materialistic bondage even for the affluent as the system creates false needs and desires in those whom it supposedly empowers. Whether one enters the world poor or affluent, one is born into a network of social relations whose power as precedent sin is overwhelming. Feminist and African-American theologians have described this precedent sin as the power of prejudice, manifesting itself in patriarchy or racism, in hateful, discriminatory attitudes and behaviors into which all are born and by which all are corrupted.[25] Invoking the work of the philosopher René Girard, James Alison has portrayed precedent, victimizing sin as the practice of scapegoating, as the violent exclusion of individuals or groups from the social body at large as a way of channeling, through focused acts of hatred, the violence that permeates the most ordinary social relations.[26]

In each of these conceptualizations, there is awareness that much of the sinning human beings do in their lives inevitably becomes social and historical. It takes shape as an evil structure, a collective precedent sin, into which the next generation is born. In such a functionalist perspective, the shared guilt of humanity is as inescapably bequeathed to every human being as it is in the classical conception of original sin. This appropriation of guilt, however, takes place both passively and actively. Guilt is *passively* appropriated as the tragic heritage of sin that every human person shares by virtue of the social dimension of his or her humanity. Guilt is *actively* appropriated as every person embraces the victimizing heritage of passive guilt. Every person born a victim is also born a future victimizer who, to a greater or lesser degree, propagates the history of sin that precedes individual sinning. By doing so, each person's sinning perversely creates the victimizing corporate sin into which the next generation is born and by which the next generation is seduced into participation.

This functionalist understanding of original sin can still be told through the Genesis story of Adam and Eve, although it need not regard the story as an account of actual historical events. Moreover, it can appreciate the intent of the traducianist explanation, which affirms the inescapability of sin by placing it in the biological makeup of every person. In measuring the faithfulness of the functionalist understanding, though, we must ask whether it accounts for both the universality of sin and the utter human need for divine grace as effectively as the traditional doctrine does. On the first count, it seems that my functionalist view is up to the task, since it insists that precedent sin is inescapable both as a matter of birth and in the way precedent sin enters every life so that all become sinners. One may object that a functionalist view, with its rather pragmatic attention to actual human behavior, leaves room for the possibility for any human life to be above sin. The Council of Trent, we saw, rejects this view in its teaching that Adam's sin "is communicated to all . . . by propagation not by imitation." The functionalist position sketched above insists with the tradition that sin is irresistible and compelling in every life, even if it prefers an existentialist to a biological (and finally metaphysical) description of how this is so. On the second count, the functionalist view's strong sense for the universality and inescapability of sin is itself an affirmation of the utter need on the part of fallen humanity for God's saving grace. Without grace, the spiral of passive and active guilt would hold humanity relentlessly in its sway, and the power of suffering that guilt brings to every life would perdure, unchallenged by God's redemptive love.

My functionalist reconstruction of the doctrine of original sin, however, parts company with the traditional understanding

of original sin on two crucial issues. It does not explain death as
divine retribution, and it does not understand the universality of
sin and guilt to entail the rejection of innocent suffering. These
positions are deeply related. The traditional doctrine of original
sin regards God's death-dealing justice as the marker of sin's universality, a universality so rife with guiltiness that innocent suffering is banished from the created and fallen world. The
thorough guiltiness of all suffering assures human responsibility
for all the evil of the world and guarantees God's innocence even
though God directly or indirectly wills suffering and death into
human life. As we might expect, the two premises that have
guided our theological inquiry are deeply related too. If God is
not the cause of death in any way, and if death is not divine retribution, then there is no need to secure God's innocence by positing a human guilt so complete that innocent suffering becomes a
theological impossibility. Whether parsed traditionally or recon-
structively, the doctrine of original sin has tremendous consequences for the doctrine of God, just as the doctrine of God has
tremendous consequences for the doctrine of original sin.

The tradition's reluctance to allow a place for innocent suffering in a Christian worldview stems from the burden that it
places on God's omnipotence and justice, as these divine attributes are traditionally conceived and imagined to be at work in a
fallen creation. If, however, we understand God's omnipotent
power over death to be exercised most fully in the resurrection
and not at all in punishment, then innocent suffering no longer
presents a scandal to God's own just actions. Indeed, if God does
not wield retributive power, then the traditional manner of speaking of God's justice becomes meaningless. My reconstructive proposal suggests that all divine power exercised in God's mighty
deeds is providentially disposed toward the healing of a fallen
humanity. All divine acts, in other words, are acts of grace. Grace,
which is all that God does, heals the universal sin and guilt, the
original sin, into which all persons are born and whose terrible
heritage every person promulgates in his or her own sinful acts.
Yet there is no reason to think that this universality of sin and
guilt, which establishes the absolute need for grace on the part of
fallen humanity, is a universal guiltiness so thick that innocent

suffering disappears in the fallen realm. According to traditional assumptions, guilty suffering subverts innocent suffering. According to the reconstructive assumptions proposed here, innocent suffering takes place amidst the guilty suffering that all undergo through their active participation in original sin's ongoing corruption of right relationship to God.

Such a stance allows innocent suffering to appear on the theological landscape and, with it, the faithful affirmation of what emotion and reason regard as a kind of moral common sense. Nevertheless, and in spite of this consistency between common experience and the claims of faith, the appearance of innocent suffering on the theological landscape shifts its customary contours in ways that seem to make familiar ground into a foreign land. The strangeness of our claim, measured against the backdrop of traditional assumptions, can be expressed in two questions. How could the extensiveness of human guilt in the understanding of original sin sketched above allow for the possibility of innocent suffering at all? And how could an omnipotent God remain innocent before, and yet present to, the innocent suffering of the world? My answer to the first question will bring this section to a close. The chapter's final section addresses the second question.

My efforts to develop a doctrine of original sin without divine retribution and with regard for innocent suffering have not compromised the Christian tradition's insistence on humanity's utter need of God's saving grace. My functionalist understanding of original sin affirms the traditional teaching on a precedent sin that precedes sinning. It regards the power of that sin as irresistible not only as the corporate guilt of humanity but also in the powerful effects of that guilt in shaping every person into an agent of sin. Guilt, the proposal insists, pervades the fallen world. The traditional doctrine of original sin denies the existence of innocent suffering within this guilty realm, since it aligns death as divine retribution with the guilt of all and measures God's absolute innocence by the absoluteness of human guilt. Free of this traditional alignment and measurement, a theology can entertain the value of real human innocence and, more, innocence in suffering amidst the tragic proportions of human sin and guilt.

No longer called upon to safeguard God's omnipotent innocence, the portrayal of the universality of guilt offered here can
admit of relative states of human innocence that emerge through
the victimization of sin, and in spite of the fact that those who are
innocent in some respects are thoroughly guilty in others. As I
noted in chapter 1, the judgment of innocent suffering does not
require the guiltlessness of the sufferer, as the traditional doctrine presupposes. When the suffering a person endures is judged
to be out of all proportion to whatever suffering the person may
have caused, the victimized sufferer suffers innocently. Innocent
suffering is unjust suffering. Without the onus of a divine, retributive justice that balances its scales with the weight of human suffering, innocent suffering becomes as common as human
injustice. Its prevalence within the universality of human sin and
guilt is, in many respects, a function of the prevalence of sin and
guilt, which themselves often cause innocent suffering.

Innocent suffering is caused by the unjust actions of persons,
but not exclusively so. Much of the innocent suffering that human
persons endure derives from the mortality that is part and parcel
of finite existence, and that is beyond the power of human
actions. In this respect, one can speak of the innocent suffering of
the young person who dies in the throes of a terminal disease
occasioned by no human action; of the family of this person, who
all innocently suffer this terrible loss; of the innocent suffering
brought on by emotional and physical incapacities; of the innocent suffering of the elderly, whose increasing age and frailty are
accompanied by increasing loneliness and bodily pain; of the
innocent suffering that accompanies any death not the result of
self-destructive behavior. In a traditional frame of reference,
humanity in original sin is responsible for all such evil that God
brings about as divine punishment. Here the deathliness of finite
existence is guilty through and through. My proposal, however,
regards such suffering as innocent whenever it is disproportionate to the guilt that persons accrue through their actions. This
measure of innocent suffering is not, of course, a specific calculus
applied in particular circumstances to determine whether or not
suffering is truly innocent. It is, rather, a general theological judg-

ment about a kind of suffering that the Christian doctrinal tradition denies.

I shall use the term "precedent evil" to describe the mortality of human finitude that transcends human power and brings innocent suffering to human lives, and distinguish that term and its referent from "precedent sin." Precedent sin is evil that human persons enact and that meets the next generation as a co-opting heritage of sin and guilt. Although precedent sin is action that all do and that makes all guilty, it is also, in the experience of its victims, one source of the innocent suffering that besets the world. Precedent evil does not refer to death itself, but to the effects that the condition of deathliness brings into life, both capriciously and predictably. Precedent evil is "precedent" by virtue of the givenness of such deathliness to the human condition. It is evil in the manner that its suffering devastatingly enters human lives, both directly for the person who suffers and dies and indirectly in the lives of those close to the sufferer who are scarred by the suffering and death of someone close. Precedent evil is not sin, since it is not willed by personal agency, either human or divine. But like sin, it can be judged to be evil in the effects its power has on human lives and even though no person wills these effects. Human persons who inevitably encounter its power judge precedent evil to be a second source of innocent suffering. In some respects, precedent evil presents a greater challenge than precedent sin to God's innocence and goodness in the face of evil. The remainder of the chapter will examine more closely God's relationship to the innocent suffering caused by precedent sin and precedent evil.

Rethinking God's Presence to Evil

I return to the question posed earlier: How could an omnipotent God remain innocent before, and present to, the innocent suffering that permeates the world? Our distinction between precedent sin and precedent evil provides a point of departure for an answer.

The classical Christian tradition does not recognize a distinction between precedent sin and precedent evil. What I have called
"precedent evil" is but an aspect of the traditional legal explanation. It is God's retributive response to the precedence of original
sin, understood as a biological inheritance. Death and suffering,
in these assumptions, are not evil but rather God's justice toward
the human guilt incurred in original sin. The classical tradition
attributes all guilt to humanity and all innocence to God. Our distinction allows for a different explanation. All human beings
stand guilty of precedent sin as inheritors of a sinful history that
shapes their own lives as sinners who act contrary to God's will for
creation. Yet the enactment of sin ever causes innocent suffering.
Victimizing sin often causes victimization out of all proportion to
the victim's guilt, and thus the scandal of innocent suffering that
the classical tradition works so hard to deny. The extent of guilt
in the account of original sin offered here implies that innocent
suffering abounds nearly as much as sin abounds. The great
depths of sin and guilt have similar depths in innocent suffering.

In this light, the issue of God's relationship to the world's suffering becomes even more pointed than in the legal explanation.
Many may find the legal explanation's denial of innocent suffering to be problematic, even to the point of a callous insensitivity.
But the denial, affirmed throughout much of the Christian tradition, eliminates the scandal of an apparently innocent suffering
before God's omnipotence. Within the boundaries of its own
explanation, the traditional doctrine never has to address the
question of why God allows the innocent to suffer, since innocent
suffering, it holds, does not occur. To the degree that my proposal
embraces innocent suffering as a moral fact, the scandalous character of such suffering touches God's goodness and power in ways
the world's suffering simply does not in the traditional doctrine.

One might think that God's relation to innocent suffering
could be explained satisfactorily by drawing on our functionalist
doctrine of original sin. Through precedent sin, human beings
are responsible for much of the world's innocent suffering, a position that seems to raise God above the scandalous fray. Human
guilt for innocent suffering, however, does not explain how God's
omnipotence could nevertheless allow innocent suffering to

occur through evil human actions. Moreover, human sin does not account for all innocent suffering. Much innocent suffering issues from precedent evil, for which no person, human or divine, bears responsibility. This kind of innocent suffering seems to present special difficulties for a coherent account of God's relation to evil. We can identify two troublesome issues in this regard. First, it seems strange to say that innocent suffering stems from precedent evil, since such evil has no moral agency as its cause. As we have seen in our first two chapters, speaking of innocence and guilt makes no sense apart from a context of moral agency. Death beyond the power of human persons and not willed by the divine person, it would seem, could not be guilty and so could not cause *innocent* suffering. Second, even if one could speak of innocent suffering caused by precedent evil, one would still need to explain why God's gracious omnipotence allows such innocent suffering to occur. Let us address these concerns in order, and by doing so bring our chapter to a close.

My theological proposal removes God's agency from suffering and death in order to reject any notion that these events are God's retributive justice and the traditional belief that all human suffering is guilty. This explanation, of course, does not mean that all personal agency is removed from suffering and death. Human persons cause much of the world's suffering and death, and in doing so they are the guilty perpetrators of much of the innocent suffering that their fellow human persons endure. This alignment of guilty perpetrator and innocent sufferer in the realm of human persons establishes a framework for the way we think about guilt and innocence. Our expectation is that someone's innocence requires someone's guilt, and, more specifically, that someone's innocent suffering requires someone's evil agency. These are the assumptions that shape the theology of divine retribution and the traditional doctrine of original sin. If the suffering and death that transcend human power and responsibility are *not* divine retribution for human guilt, then God, it seems, must be a guilty perpetrator, since only God could wield this kind of power. This, however, is an untenable thought for Christian belief. There is, though, another way to construe these matters so that divine retribution and God's innocence are not the only compatible assumptions in Christian explanation. I suggested the lines of such an explanation at the close of chapter 2.

Innocent suffering need not be causally aligned to guilty agency in order to acquire its integrity. Innocent or guilty suffering requires a moral context of persons in relationship if suffering is to be raised above the amoral realm of nonpersonal beings. There is no innocent suffering in the animal world. And there is no innocent suffering in a godless world when human persons are not the guilty perpetrators of suffering. Christians, however, affirm the existence of a personal God who is present to all creation, and so certainly to the moral community of innocent and guilty persons. This moral community is not composed of self-contained relationships in which guilt or innocence might appear depending on actions that ensue in the relations between one person and another. Personal relationships are not isolated engagements. They are, instead, part of an extraordinarily complex web of relations that make up the moral community considered as a whole.

Within this web, guilty perpetrator and innocent sufferer are not the only moral roles available to human persons. Human persons also find themselves standing as witnesses to guilty victimization and innocent suffering. This witnessing can be an apathetic regard toward innocent suffering, itself a guilty action. Sometimes moral witnessing appears as sympathy that yet is really helpless before the scandal of innocent suffering, since such suffering can be so pervasive or distant or irresistible. Witnessing to innocent suffering becomes an ethical activity that can be accomplished in any number of ways—as resistance to the perpetrator, as comfort to the sufferer, or as the reform of communal conditions that enabled or even encouraged guilty victimization to occur. The particular relationship between guilty agent and innocent sufferer is one aspect of life in the moral community, and one with which the justice system of any society is especially concerned. This relationship, however, is not what determines a moral context. Witnessing as sympathetic regard and as active engagement are forms of solidarity with innocent suffering that extend the lines of moral relationship far beyond the tragic partnership of guilty perpetrator and innocent sufferer. The presence

of sympathetic and engaged witnesses to innocent suffering testifies to its scandalous nature. Their witnessing in many respects
establishes the character of moral community. Their shared judgment about the innocence of the victim and the guilt of the perpetrator shapes the community's most basic sensibilities about
virtue and vice. Members of the larger moral community who witness through Christian eyes find that their shared judgment about
the innocence of the victim and the guilt of the perpetrator
shapes their most basic sensibilities about grace and sin, about
God's saving power and the depth of human need.

The divine person is not a stranger to the moral community
in which innocent suffering sadly flourishes. Indeed, we would do
well to conceive God's omnipresence as a moral witness to innocent suffering. Whereas the classical tradition makes extraordinary efforts to distance God completely from innocent suffering
by denying its very existence, my proposal insists on both the
moral fact of innocent suffering and on God's unbounded inti-
macy to the kind of suffering that makes the history of sin so egregious and death's effects so rampant. God's presence testifies to
the guilt of the perpetrator and stands in solidarity with the victim. We can speak of God's solidarity with suffering as a divine
sympathy, as have several Christian thinkers, and as long as God's
presence to innocent suffering is not represented as a caring,
though helpless, compassion. God's sympathetic presence is
never helpless. Believers in the biblical promise hold that God's
presence is always engaged, and effectively so, in the defeat of
suffering and death, which beset both the innocent victim and the
guilty perpetrator alike. In God's saving omnipresence, sympathy
and engagement are the one, same divine activity.

God's presence fills up the created space occupied by guilty
perpetrator and innocent sufferer. All who are born and live
under the power of original sin stand at once guilty and innocent
before God, and all of God's being is disposed toward the destruction of the suffering and death caused by the guiltiness of human
sinning. God's witnessing omnipresence extends also to innocent
suffering not caused by personal agency, suffering that my proposal has refused to regard as divine retribution. If the witnessing
presence of persons is what establishes a moral community in

which both guilt and innocence appear, then even suffering and death beyond personal agency can be judged innocent by such a community, as long as the suffering is disproportionate to the guilt that any human person bears. Within this community, God's omnipresent witnessing is particularly important, not only because it sets a moral standard of judgment and solidarity to which all persons are responsible but also because only God's witness, as sympathetic engagement, is able to transcend the final powerlessness of other persons in the moral community and resist the powers of suffering and death. The witnessing of all persons, human and divine, provides a moral context in which so-called natural suffering can be judged innocent. But God's unique witnessing within that community, as an engaged omnipresence enacting the divine promise to destroy all death, raises so-called natural suffering from a state of amorality to a state of innocence.

Aside from its untraditional character, this explanation seems odd because it asks us to imagine innocent suffering without a guilty, and so personal, cause. Recent theological reconstructions of the doctrine of original sin often avoid this apparent inconsistency by arguing that death not caused by guilty human action is natural, and, as natural, its effects in themselves are neither guilty nor innocent. Karl Rahner develops a theology of original sin along these lines by proposing that only our own guilt, caused by the distortion of personal sin, leads us to view the naturalness of death as something threatening. For Rahner, death should not be threatening. Indeed, he claims, the radical limit it places on human existence is necessary for the exercise of real freedom and personal decision that allows persons to reach their own moral determination.[27] My proposal has not adopted this approach, which is favored by many modern theologians. To regard death as natural places it in God's creative plan and immediately subsumes death under God's providence. Death becomes something that God wills and, as providence, something that an omnipotent God does at least indirectly in the circumstances of every death. My reading of scripture and tradition uncovers a God who is an enemy of suffering and death. Suffering and death are powers God has vowed finally to destroy, and God is omnipotently engaged now in that saving activity. Even though suffering and death are not personal powers, and so not guilty agents, they yet cause suffering judged to be innocent in the community of moral witness that itself has natural and supernatural proportions.[28]

Juridical assumptions so shape our ethical thinking that we are unaccustomed to the idea of suffering in the moral realm for which *someone* is neither guilty nor responsible. The traditional legal explanation accepts the juridical model, making Adam, Eve, and, indirectly, all their children responsible for the death God brings about as punishment for sin. Even Rahner's existentialist reinterpretation of the doctrine of original sin, which makes death part of the natural order, finds it difficult to escape the juridical assumptions it criticizes. For Rahner, false fears about death stemming from their own sin and guilt cause human persons to suffer in the face of natural death, a position that ironically attributes deathly suffering to personal guilt even as it rejects the traditional teaching that sin causes death. My proposal departs from the juridical alignment of guilty action to innocent suffering by suggesting that there is tragic suffering caused by no guilty person that yet can be judged innocent in the moral community of persons. There is Christian tragedy in which suffering is inescapable because of the guilty history of precedent sin. And there is Christian tragedy in which innocent suffering is caused by no action of an immoral perpetrator. What makes this suffering tragic is the inevitability of its evil in our lives, and its insidious power to enter our lives in crushing, dehumanizing ways that thwart every real exercise of freedom and decision.[29] God stands on the side of innocent suffering that is caused by precedent sin. And God also stands on the side of innocent suffering that is caused by precedent evil. In doing so, God does not stand opposed to a death worked into the created order as God's own providential design, but rather to the deathliness that enters human lives as a subversion of God's life-sharing purposes.

How, then, are we to imagine God's omnipresence to a created order through which precedent evil courses? Conceptualizing God's relation to precedent evil seems to be a fruitless or even nonsensical endeavor, since it involves conceiving God's relation to a power that God did not create and that exceeds the capacity of the human will. Precedent evil is not the result of volition. Its power to devastate lives is not the consequence of moral failure. This idea of a free-standing power that works evil in human lives, a power about whose origins we can only remain agnostic, seems to be incapable of assimilation in an orthodox Christian world-view in which God's creative energies are the source of all creaturely power. Perhaps, in spite of my best intentions, I have arrived at the dualism I was willing to risk but not endorse. Perhaps, in the context of Christian assumptions, it is not possible to imagine deathly power that is not finally wielded by God either as retribution or as providence. Developing a detailed account of God's relation to precedent evil would require time and space beyond the capacity of the present study. There are, however, ways in which God's relation to precedent evil can be productively conceived, so that dualism is avoided and God's retributive or providential power is withdrawn from death. Two examples will have to suffice.

In many respects, the problem of conceiving God's hostile relation to precedent evil resembles the problem of conceiving the real integrity of a created world different from God, in which purposes other than God's can emerge and transpire at all. Jürgen Moltmann has called attention to the Jewish kabbalistic doctrine of *zimzum* as a resource for a Christian theology of creation that addresses this problem. Theologically understood, *zimzum* refers to God's own willed act of self-limitation in creating the world. The creation of what is truly creaturely, of what is not-God, leads God to will the negative precondition of created being, the nothingness from which creation is drawn. God retreats into God's own self, drawing a line, so to speak, between God's presence and its absence. "God," Moltmann speculates, "makes room for his creation by withdrawing his presence."[30] The divine *zimzum* is not yet creation but rather a *nihil* to be filled by the somethingness of God's life-giving creation. And yet, as God's willed withdrawal, this *nihil* is a disturbing, anomic "place" that ripples with the divine absence:

> The space which comes into being and is set free by God's self-limitation is a literally God-forsaken space. The *nihil* in which God creates his creation is God-forsakenness, hell, absolute

death; and it is against the threat of this that he maintains his
creation in life.[31]

At its worst, this theology of creation could be understood to support a divinely willed dualism in which demonic forces are
unleashed, however indirectly, by the divine will or in which
God's creative hands are tied by the necessity of negatively willing
precedent evil as a backdrop for the positive act of creating the
world. Moltmann, however, proposes a more constructive interpretation of the divine *zimzum* that accords with my theological
proposal. God's "creative activity outwards," he suggests, "is preceded by [a] humble divine self-restriction." This divine act of
humility, finally a divine act of love, is what makes creation possible. It is a divine "letting-be" or "making room" that takes the otherness of creation seriously.[32] The power of death may course
through that otherness, but not as a power that God wills in any
way and to which God ever remains opposed.

Elizabeth Johnson offers the possibility of another conceptualization in line with the worldview of contemporary physics.[33]
Quantum theory represents the micro world of subatomic particles as sheer randomness and indeterminacy utterly unconstrained by the Newtonian laws that rule in the macro world of
predictable cause and effect. Chance, rather than organization,
governs reality at its most basic level. Theologians have long recognized the challenge quantum indeterminacy presents to the
traditional understanding of divine providence, which sees creation charged with divine purpose, design, and direction. Johnson argues for an understanding of God's providence that can be
reconciled with the chance thoroughly at work in the subatomic
world and, by extension, throughout the sensible world. In doing
so, she finds Aquinas's conception of secondary causality still to
have resiliency in accounting for randomness in nature. For
Aquinas, God's providence does not ordinarily appear in the
world as an interruption of the natural laws. Rather, God's activity is mediated "secondarily," in and through nature's own created activity. Secondary causality does not entail God's
imposition of necessity on the activity of nature through which
God works. Contingency is a dimension of the natural order and

so too a medium of the divine activity. Aquinas, of course, never imagined the sort of contingency in nature envisioned in quantum theory. Nevertheless, Johnson judges that Thomistic secondary causality can be made to apply to the quantum world "with almost surprising ease."[34]

The prevalence of randomness in what Christians affirm as the created world, Johnson proposes, points toward God's purposeful creation of randomness as a dimension of the matter and energy that make up the physical universe. This randomness is an ever-present feature even of the laws of nature that capture the predictable behavior of the current moment in the history of cosmic evolution. Randomness, though, is an essential, albeit unpredictable, ingredient in the evolutionary movement from which the present universe came to be. "'In the beginning,'" Johnson argues,

> the Creator endows the material of this world with one set of potentialities rather than another. These are then unveiled by chance exploring their gamut in an inevitable yet indeterminate evolutionary process. Indeed, in retrospect, this seems to be the only way in which all of matter's potentialities might eventually, given enough time and space, be actualized. Consequently, chance is not an alternative to law, but the very means by which law is creative.[35]

Randomness becomes one important way in which God's providence is at work in secondary causality. For Johnson, this providence is not coercive or overwhelming. Indeed, if God has created a world so thoroughly shot through with indeterminacy and chance, then God risks much by making a world so open to possibility, a world that could have evolved at all of its levels in many possible ways. "Exercising this power," Johnson concludes, "God's providential guidance eschews pre-ordaining or imposing exact sequences of events but rather makes itself known as the patient, subtle presence of a gracious Creator who achieves divine purpose through the free play of created processes."[36]

Whereas Johnson is interested in reconciling providence and chance, we are interested here in conceiving God's omnipresence to a created order in which precedent evil abounds. Johnson's theological reflections on creation can be helpful in this regard. She portrays chance as a creaturely reality with an integrity of its own that God respects. By analogy, chance might be imagined as inanimate matter's free choice, a free choice that exists in the same space as God's omnipotence while not being compelled by it. The analogy holds to the degree that matter's indeterminacy, like human free choice, is not governed by necessity, even the necessity identified with God's freedom in a traditional conception of God. The analogy breaks down, as any analogy must, at the point that it seems to ascribe mind and will to what are only blind forces. Particles in the quantum world do not choose freely in the way human persons do. Yet, if Johnson's proposal for understanding creation is sound, then in its broad lines of explanation we have a way of imagining how precedent evil could possess such power in a world created by the divine omnipotence and yet not issue from God's will. Precedent evil, we could say, is the prevailing, random consequence of an evolutionary process that the omnipotent God risked and with which the same God of life is eternally disappointed.

Both explanations considered above show that any effort to imagine the origin of precedent evil involves thinking the thought of things outside God that possess the power to work against the divine purposes. Christian traditions that affirm human free choice of the will before or after the Fall (nearly all!) have always made such a thought the basis of their claims about precedent sin, at its worst a deathly power that free choice brings into the world. One might say that these traditions risk a dualism in some small way, at least to the degree that evil arises at all in a world created thoroughly good by a good God. Imagining the natural world as a thing outside God that possesses the power to work against the divine purposes—as in the mystical notion of *zimzum* or in Johnson's efforts to accommodate the evidence of modern physics to God's creative activity—increases the risk of dualism by attributing to the natural world a kind of God-resisting autonomy, albeit without free choice of the will. But as much as this conceptualization risks dualism, it does not lose its hold on a traditional nondualism, while gaining all the advantages of a nonretributive understanding of God's relation to suffering and death.

Our earlier discussion concluded that the question of God's

power toward evil is not productively answered through a theodicy but through a theological interpretation of scripture and tradition, specifically one that highlights God's revealed promise to defeat all death. Christians believe that this revealed promise is made by a God who is engaged even now in the defeat of suffering and death and whose completion of this saving task will bring about the destruction of all death. For believers, God's omnipotence is not (or at least should not be) a formal capacity that stands juxtaposed, theoretically and abstractly, to the world's suffering. Such a formal capacity is envisaged whenever God's relation to evil is configured as God's "allowance" of evil, an allowance that renders God's goodness questionable. Theodicists may seek a logical solution to a logically defined problem of how God's power can be reconciled with suffering. From the standpoint of faith, however, God's power is not merely an infinite ability that might be applied in one way or another and suffering is not one term in a logical dilemma. Within the circle of faith, both innocent and guilty suffering are the very condition of a fallen humanity that stands in utter need of God's saving grace. And God's unlimited power is the divine love that, as grace, is utterly disposed toward healing all the guilty and innocent suffering that precedent sin and precedent evil bring to human life. These claims in faith are made on the basis of actual experiences of need, hope, and reconciliation that are formed in an existential encounter with the living God, a God whose presence manifests itself in death-defeating action accomplished in every moment, even if not fully accomplished on this side of death. As we saw in the previous chapter, the only appropriate mystery of faith in God's relation to suffering is not if or how omnipotence can be justified before the world's evil but rather why God's saving omnipotence does not destroy the evil of suffering and death completely in the present moment. The "problem" of God's power and the prevalence of suffering is, for faith, not one of consistent reasoning but of human patience.

This position may seem rather cavalier from the perspective of theodicy. It seems not to present the sort of total explanation that theodicy seeks. In addition, faith's comparatively incomplete answer seems to be given with a bold confidence in God's final triumph over evil that would seem to offer little consolation to those who struggle now in the midst of precedent sin and precedent evil, especially when the struggle besets those who suffer innocently, as it often does. However bold faith's confidence in God's final triumph may be, its boldness never comes easily or cheaply. Faith is never free from the struggle of affirming God's good and saving purposes before all the fallen forces that bring suffering and death to human life. Faith, as Paul Tillich has taught so well, is never free from doubt, and this doubt is not a disposition extraneous to faith but rather a dimension of the struggle that every real act of faith continually requires.[37] Faith too, as Charles Péguy has taught equally well, is largely a matter of hope.[38] Its affirmation of trust in God testifies not only to what God is doing now but also to what God will bring about in a future filled with the realization of God's purposes. The patience required of faith is its appropriate response to faith's ongoing struggle with evil, as well as to God's ongoing struggle with evil in which faith believes and hopes. It is patience in the expectation of God's final victory over evil. It is not patience in coming to understand God's purposes in death.

Notes

1. For a discussion of the workings of tradition, see John E. Thiel, *Senses of Tradition: Continuity and Development in Catholic Faith* (New York: Oxford University Press, 2000).

2. The works of Karl Barth and Hans Urs von Balthasar provide good examples of this theological style.

3. The works of Friedrich Schleiermacher and Karl Rahner provide good examples of this theological style.

4. See *Adam and Eve: Jewish, Christian, and Muslim Readings on Genesis and Gender,* ed. K. Kvam et al. (Bloomington, Ind.: Indiana University Press, 1999), 44.

5. Elaine Pagels, *Adam, Eve, and the Serpent* (New York: Random House, 1988), 146. Pagels makes this point with regard to Augustine's stance on original sin, though her observation applies just as much to Paul's claim that sin causes death.

6. Augustine, *On Free Choice of the Will*, trans. A. Benjamin and L. H. Hackstaff (Indianapolis, Ind.: Bobbs-Merrill, 1964), 18–22.

7. Augustine, *Confessions*, trans. R. S. Pine-Coffin (New York: Penguin Books, 1961), 28 (I, 7).

8. Ibid., 47 (II, 4).

9. Ibid., 123 (VI, 8).

10. Pelagius, "Letter to Demetrias," in *Theological Anthropology*, ed. and trans. J. P. Burns (Philadelphia: Fortress Press, 1981), 41.

11. Augustine, *On the Grace of Christ, and On Original Sin*, in *Saint Augustine: Anti-Pelagian Writings*, Nicene and Post-Nicene Fathers 5, trans. P. Holmes et al. (Grand Rapids: Wm. B. Eerdmans, 1978), 253.

12. St. Augustine, *City of God*, trans. H. Bettenson (New York: Penguin Books, 1986), 577 (XIV, 16).

13. Ibid. Augustine articulates this position in several writings. See, for example, Augustine, *The Literal Meaning of Genesis*, vol. 2, trans. J. Taylor, S.J. (New York: Newman Press, 1982), 80f.

14. See J. N. D. Kelly, *Early Christian Doctrines* (San Francisco: Harper & Row, 1978), 345. Elaine Pagels is far less tentative than Kelly in finding a traducianist position in Augustine, at least with respect to the communication of original sin. See Pagels, *Adam, Eve, and the Serpent*, 109.

15. See Peter Brown, *The Body and Society: Men, Women, and Sexual Renunciation in Early Christianity* (New York: Columbia University Press, 1988), 408.

16. Augustine expounds this position in several writings. See, for example, *On Grace and Free Will* and *On the Predestination of the Saints*, in *Saint Augustine: Anti-Pelagian Writings*, 443–65, 497–519.

17. Henricus Denzinger-Adolfus Schönmetzer, *Enchiridion Symbolorum Definitionem et Declarationem de Rebus Fidei et Morum*, 34th ed. (Freiburg im Breisgau: Herder, 1967), 137, no. 397. English translation from *The Church Teaches: Documents of the Church in English Translation*, trans. J. F. Clarkson, S.J., et al. (St. Louis: B. Herder, 1955), 228.

18. In the following passage from *On the Soul and Its Origin*, for example, Augustine articulates his understanding of the church's teaching, which he specifically ascribes to Paul: ". . . the apostle has most plainly taught us: That owing to one man all pass into condemnation who are born of Adam unless they are born again in Christ, even as He has appointed them to be regenerated, before they die in the body, whom he predestinated to everlasting life, as the most merciful bestower of grace; whilst to those whom he has predestinated to eternal death, He is also the most righteous awarder of punishment, not only on account of the sins which they add in the indulgence of their own will, but also because of their original sin, even if, as in the case of infants, they add nothing thereto" (Augustine, *On the Soul and Its Origin*, in *Saint Augustine: Anti-Pelagian Writings*, 361).

19. Denzinger-Schönmetzer, *Enchiridion Symbolorum*, 369, no. 1521; *The Church Teaches*, 230.

20. Denzinger-Schönmetzer, *Enchiridion Symbolorum*, 367, no. 1513; 366, no. 1511; *The Church Teaches*, 159, 158. The clarity of this conciliar teaching, based on centuries-old precedents, makes it difficult to understand Edward Schillebeeckx's claim that "Christianity does not give any explanation for suffering, but demonstrates a way of life" (Edward Schillebeeckx, *Christ: The Experience of Jesus as Lord*, trans. J. Bowden [New York: Crossroad, 1981], 699).

21. Denzinger-Schönmetzer, *Enchiridion Symbolorum*, 367–68, no. 1515; *The Church Teaches*, 160.

22. Augustine, *The Confessions of St. Augustine*, trans. J. K. Ryan (Garden City, N.Y.: Doubleday, 1960), 84 (III, 6).

23. Elizabeth A. Dreyer, *Earth Crammed with Heaven: A Spirituality of Everyday Life* (New York: Paulist Press, 1994), 114–35.

24. See, for example, Gustavo Gutiérrez, *A Theology of Liberation: History, Politics, Salvation*, trans. C. Inda and J. Eagleson (Maryknoll, N.Y.: Orbis Books, 1988); idem, *We Drink from Our Own Wells: The Spiritual Journey of a People*, trans. M. O'Connell (Maryknoll, N.Y.: Orbis Books, 1984). See also Dorothee Soelle, *Suffering*, trans. E. Kalin (Philadelphia: Fortress Press, 1975).

25. Among the many possible citations, see, for example, Anne E. Carr, *Transforming Grace: Christian Tradition and Women's Experience* (San Francisco: HarperSanFrancisco, 1990), 21–59; Rosemary Radford Ruether, *Sexism and God-Talk: Toward a Feminist Theology* (Boston: Beacon Press, 1983), 159–92; James H. Evans, Jr., *We Have Been Believers: An African-American Systematic Theology* (Minneapolis: Fortress Press, 1992), 104–7; *A Troubling in My Soul: Womanist Perspectives on Evil and Suffering*, ed. E. Townes (Maryknoll, N.Y.: Orbis Books, 1993).

26. James Alison, *The Joy of Being Wrong: Original Sin Through Easter Eyes* (New York: Crossroad, 1998).

27. Karl Rahner, *Foundations of Christian Faith: An Introduction to the Idea of Christianity*, trans. W. Dych (New York: Seabury Press, 1978), 115; idem, "Ideas for a Theology of Death," in *Theological Investigations*, vol. 13, trans. C. Ernst (New York: Seabury Press, 1975), 180.

28. I should note that there are some similarities between my proposal and the soteriology constructed by Edward Schillebeeckx. See Edward Schillebeeckx, *Christ: The Experience of Jesus as Lord*, trans. J. Bowden (New York: Crossroad, 1981), 724–839.

29. Cf. the discussion of tragedy as a theological category in Kathleen M. Sands, *Escape from Paradise: Evil and Tragedy in Feminist Theology* (Minneapolis: Fortress Press, 1994), 1–16. On the same theological theme, see also Wendy Farley, *Tragic Vision and Divine Compassion: A*

Contemporary Theodicy (Louisville, Ky.: Westminster/John Knox Press, 1990); Edward Farley, *Good and Evil: Interpreting the Human Condition* (Minneapolis: Fortress Press, 1990). It is interesting to note that these three authors enlist the category of tragedy to serve theological proposals not committed to a personal conception of God, assuming, perhaps, that the category of tragedy especially serves a theological program not beholden to this sort of traditional theism. I have proposed a notion of theological tragedy that portrays the personal God's relationship to precedent sin and precedent evil.

30. Jürgen Moltmann, *God in Creation: A New Theology of Creation and the Spirit of God,* trans. M. Kohl (San Francisco: HarperSanFrancisco, 1991), 87.

31. Ibid., 87–88.

32. Ibid., 88.

33. Elizabeth A. Johnson, C.S.J., "Does God Play Dice? Divine Providence and Chance," *Theological Studies* 57 (1996): 3–18.

34. Ibid., 14.

35. Ibid., 15.

36. Ibid., 17.

37. Paul Tillich, *Dynamics of Faith* (New York: Harper & Row, 1957), 16–22.

38. Charles Péguy, *The Portal of the Mystery of Hope,* trans. D. Schindler, Jr. (Grand Rapids: William B. Eerdmans, 1996).

∻ 5 ∻

Acting Innocently

CONSEQUENCES FOR CHRISTOLOGY

AND DISCIPLESHIP

MUCH OF OUR THEOLOGICAL REFLECTION on God and evil has been a matter of finding an adequate way to imagine what faith truly believes about God. Believers claim to know about God in several ways. Scripture and tradition are extraordinary ways of knowing about God. In the different Christian churches, in somewhat different respects, believers claim that scripture and tradition are inspired conveyors of God's truth, which is always a saving truth. Scripture and tradition are God's own revelation about Godself to humanity. In these pages I have tried to take the authority of God's revelation seriously by showing how a particular reading of the entire biblical story and a particular understanding of God's battle with evil from ancient tradition encourage us to think of God's relation to evil in a certain manner.

Scripture and tradition, however, even as God's revelation, are not self-standing communicators of information to a passively receptive community of faith. The wider life experience of believers always provides an active setting for the reception of God's revelation. Experience shapes and molds the ways in which the truth of God's revelation is encountered in any life, in any time and place. Moreover, experience itself is a medium of God's truth. Even though experience does not enjoy the privileged sta-

143

tus of divine revelation, and even though experience can be thoroughly false, its apprehension of God's truth can be just as authentic as the most time-honored claims of faith, even when the present claims of faith seem novel. The theological truthfulness of experience finally is a matter of whether experience has really apprehended God's Spirit, the Truth itself who is present to all persons, times, and places.

My theological proposal has argued from the truth of experience in order to construct an understanding of God and evil consistent with the evidence of scripture and tradition. The proposal has recognized the truth of innocent suffering to which common experience testifies. It has acknowledged the offense caused to many believers by the popular belief that God's good purposes are woven into the suffering and death that often devastate human lives. The evidence of these truthful experiences has led us to reinterpret the claims of traditional doctrine. Thus far in our presentation, the results have been a conception of God that places providence completely on the side of God's life-giving power, utterly opposed to the deathly powers that beset the created world, and a conception of original sin that rejects the idea of divine retribution as God's just response to sin.

The novel claim for the truth of innocent suffering before God has implications for other central themes in the system of Christian belief. Two, in particular, merit our attention. First, I shall consider the implications of a theology of innocent suffering for Christology, the theological explanation of the person and work of Jesus Christ, whom Christians believe to be "God . . . with us" (Matthew 1:23). For Christians, Jesus is the incarnate presence of God who brings salvation to the world. His person and work as the savior will have a bearing on how we understand the innocent suffering that, I have maintained, does indeed stand before God. Jesus is also the model for the formation of Christian character, for the ethical obligations that Christians freely embrace in order to enact their beliefs in God, Christ, sin, and virtue. I shall conclude by examining the ethical implications of a theology of innocent suffering for the task of Christian discipleship.

Jesus in the Logic of Divine Promise

My interpretation of scripture in chapter 3 unfolded as a canonical reading of the biblical text. Canonical interpretation does not scrutinize the features of a particular passage or even of a specific book of the Bible. It does not give priority to the analytical results that the historical-critical method might bring to or glean from the text, such as its cultural background, the concerns of the author, the assumptions of the text's audience, and so forth. A canonical reading approaches the Bible from the perspective of faith, regarding it as though it were one big book, a narrative with a single plot that relates the wonders of God's saving deeds. Since this narrative is wide-ranging and full of diversity, a canonical reading directly or indirectly must convey the unity of its saving plot by appeal to one or another thematic variation that runs throughout the saving story.

My reading made much of the notion of divine promise as a way of comprehending the unity of the biblical plot.[1] Expressly at certain points in the biblical narrative and implicitly throughout its pages, God promises believers that all of God's unlimited power is now and will be devoted to the destruction of suffering and death. God's promise, like any promise, is a word offered in the face of an unseen future before which one anticipates the complete keeping of the promise. For believers, God's promising words are no less powerful than God's words that, simply by being spoken, brought about the world's creation. As words of promise that have not been fully realized, however, they require both faith and hope in their final fulfillment.

As any of us know from our own lives, promises are not made meaningfully in the abstract. They are made in a relationship of trust, loyalty, and commitment in which earlier promises have been made and kept. A promise made outside the history of such a relationship is only a promise in the most formal sense and is really judged to be no promise at all. At best, it may be the beginning of the commitment that such a promise entails. Offered outside such a history, it is only an expression of intent made by someone whose words and deeds are unproven. Christians meet

God's promise to destroy death forever as a promise that has not been fulfilled for them. Its fulfillment could only be accomplished in the eschatological event of resurrected life in which God's defeat of suffering and death is complete. On this side of resurrected life, death still stands before the believer not merely as something to be endured but as the threat of the emptiness of God's promise that must be confronted constantly in their lives and in the lives of others. Yet Christian belief affirms God's promise of the resurrection as one that is concrete and not abstract. It is a promise that has a history, for the narrated promise of the entire Bible has already been kept in a decisive way in God's resurrection of Jesus from the dead. In this respect, the promise revealed by God in the Bible is worthy of the believer's faith. It is a reliable promise because God has already shown Godself to be a keeper of such promises in raising Jesus from the dead.

Jesus' resurrection is more than God's kept promise. It is itself the most explicit way in which God makes the biblical promise to destroy suffering and death. This may seem like a strange thing to say, since Jesus' resurrection is an event and not a string of words that take a promissory form. Promises, though, are not merely spoken words. In speaking a promise, we *do* something. We pledge actions to our words so that our speaking becomes an act of commitment. But more, we are obliged to act on the promise in order to make it come true. Promises that never pass beyond words into actions echo disappointment, failure, or even betrayal in the vacuous space of their unrealized performance.

Christians believe that God makes the promise to destroy suffering and death in the revealing words of scripture. They believe that God enacts that promise in all of God's actions that embrace all times and places. Every graceful act of God brings creation closer to the fulfillment of God's biblical promise. Jesus' resurrection, though, is an extraordinary way of conveying the biblical promise, for in raising Jesus from the dead God at once makes the biblical promise as explicit as it could possibly be and shows, by the promise's enactment, how it will be kept for all. Were we to express this promising event in explicit words, we could say that in Jesus' resurrection from the dead God promises to do for humanity what God has already done to Jesus. Just as God does not leave Jesus in death but raises him from death to life, God promises in the resurrection of Jesus not to leave humanity in death but to raise humanity to life and, in doing so, to destroy all suffering and death.

From one point of view, this expression of the biblical promise and Easter hope sounds utterly Christian. Christian belief has always insisted on the closest connection between Jesus' resurrection and our own. The destruction of death that God promises to all has a primacy in God's destruction of death for Jesus. And the resurrection of the dead depends on Jesus' resurrection to such a degree that, in Paul's words, "if the dead are not raised, then Christ has not been raised. If Christ has not been raised, your faith is futile and you are still in your sins" (1 Corinthians 15:16–17). From another point of view, however, the claim that God will do to us what God did to Jesus seems an audacious way of conceiving and speaking about God's defeat of death, for it seems to press the closeness between Jesus and ourselves too far. Any action on God's part on behalf of Jesus would seem to be unique simply by virtue of the Christian claim that Jesus is the eternally divine Son of God. Jesus' divinity, in other words, seems to make him so different from us that any identity between Jesus and humanity seems to risk making too little of Jesus or too much of humanity. This risk seems especially keen in God's biblical promise conveyed in the event of Jesus' resurrection. If God's promise is to do to us what God has done to Jesus, then this close identification of Jesus' resurrection with our own might suggest that the shared consequence of God's action toward Jesus and toward humanity entails a shared condition that this action addresses—as though Jesus stood before the awesome power of death and the gratuity of the resurrection in the same powerless condition as all of humanity. And yet, as strange as it may seem to some Christian sensibilities, this powerlessness of Jesus before death is precisely what believers are obliged to affirm in faith.

That this identification with Jesus' powerlessness seems risky is a testimony to the "one-sided orthodoxy" prevalent in our Christian communities. Since the fourth-century creed of Nicaea, Christians have explicitly confessed that Jesus is "one in being" with God in divinity, but have often affirmed this faith at the expense of the equally important claim of the fifth-century creed of Chalcedon that Jesus is "one in being" with us in our humanity, and "like us in every respect except for sin."[2] The consequence of this skewed emphasis is the Christian inclination to think of the resurrection as the work of Jesus' own divine and omnipotent agency. But to deny Jesus' powerlessness before death, and so the gratuity of the resurrection even for Jesus, would deny the full humanity of the savior on which orthodox Christian belief insists. If Jesus embraces humanity fully in all respects but sin, and if humanity's powerlessness before death is neither sin nor the consequence of sin, as I have argued, then Chalcedon's rule of faith would expect Jesus' powerlessness before death to be no different from our own. In the fullness of his humanity, in the midst of his own death, Jesus stands as much in need of God's graceful power in the resurrection as any other human being.

We should understand Jesus' powerlessness before death to be the existential condition of his own innocent suffering. In this respect, the powerlessness before death Jesus shares with all humanity is, at the same time, a sharing in the innocent suffering that human persons powerlessly endure before death and the deathliness that they meet throughout their lives. Jesus, of course, is not an innocent sufferer in the same way that other human beings are. Jesus' will is not seduced by the precedent sin that courses through history, passing from generation to generation as false desires reenact the primal sin with bitter frequency. Jesus' innocent suffering is uncompromised by the guilt that humanity bears for the reception and promulgation of original sin. Although Jesus is not guilty of precedent sin, he does encounter its terrible power throughout his life, and especially in the violence of his betrayal, torture, and death. He remains an innocent sufferer before this evil of human making. He is burdened by it and struggles with it in the course of his life, and he is overwhelmed by its hateful power in his last days.

Jesus also remains an innocent sufferer before the precedent evil that he encounters in the disease, disability, emotional afflictions, and deaths of others, as well as in his own human struggle with these manifestations of precedent evil. My distinction between precedent evil and precedent sin removes human guilt from precedent evil. It disconnects suffering and death from the causality of Adam's sin and so from the agency of God's retributive justice. This distinction between precedent sin and precedent evil enables us to say with the tradition that Jesus was sinless, since he did not contribute to the history of precedent sin in any way, and yet know that, as fully human in every respect but sin, Jesus stood before precedent evil just as every human being does. Like all human beings, Jesus was beset by physical illness and by the emotional anguish of fear, anxiety, and grief stirred by the death around him and by the prospect of his own death.

This insistence that Jesus shared nonguilty suffering and death with all humanity in his encounter with precedent evil enables us to see that the traditional legal explanation is at the root of the latent monophysitism so common to Christian faith throughout its entire history. Monophysitism, the belief that Jesus was utterly divine but human only in appearance, contradicts the orthodox teaching of the church, which insists that Jesus shares the fullness of humanity in order to bring humanity to salvation. The attractiveness of monophysitism to popular piety, though, might simply reflect its consistency with the logic of divine retribution. If suffering and the existential fact of death are divine punishment for the sins of which all are guilty, then Jesus' sinlessness would require him to stand above the physical and emotional limitations that divine retribution justly brings to human life. A strong monophysitism, which denies Jesus' susceptibility to any real suffering, is difficult to hold given the way that Jesus' life ended—in excruciating torture and brutal death. A weak monophysitism is the more common form of this latent Christian belief. A weak monophysitism concedes Jesus' suffering in the passion but imagines Jesus' life before the passion to be free of suffering, brimming with the unconstrained power of his divine nature. Jesus' passion and death become the exception to the logic of retribution in this weak monophysitism because they are invested with sacrificial meaning, a point that requires our careful attention.

Innocent Suffering in the Logic
of Sacrificial Atonement

The understanding of Jesus' death as a sacrificial atonement has its origins in the earliest New Testament witness. We find its first literary expression in Paul's primitive confession of faith in 1 Corinthians 15: "For I handed on to you as of first importance what I in turn had received: that Christ died for our sins in accordance with the scriptures, and that he was buried, and that he was raised on the third day in accordance with the scriptures." Paul's testimony to the Corinthian church, which he represents as the nascent religion's oldest faith, has continued to be handed on from generation to generation as the tradition's time-honored belief. The notion of sacrificial atonement, expressed in the words "Christ died for our sins," is a compelling way to conceive of the event of the cross, and so much so that it has always fired the Christian religious imagination. This is especially true since the Middle Ages and the powerful influence of the theologian and archbishop Anselm of Canterbury (1033–1109), whose reflections on the logic of sacrificial atonement have done much to shape Christian assumptions about innocent suffering, and especially Jesus as innocent sufferer.

Anselm's most important theological treatise, *Why God Became a Human Being* (1098), attempts to demonstrate the rational coherence of God's salvation of the world through the suffering and death of Jesus, the incarnate Son of God. Anselm weaves together a number of argumentive threads—among them, legal theory, the two-natures Christology of Chalcedon, and an aesthetic understanding of creation—in order to construct a rationale for why God saved the world as God did, through Jesus' death on the cross. According to Anselm, the answer to the question Why did God become a human being? can be provided by human reason aided by faith. Sin, Anselm argues, is a disruption of the order, beauty, goodness, and truth of God's creation, a disruption caused by the arrogance of Adam's sin and the distorted rippling of that sin through the generations. Sin is an assault on God's honor that demands to be redressed, lest God's divine will and loving purposes be thwarted by the contrary power of evil.

God is aggrieved by sin, but not in some petty way, as though God's wounded pride demanded a face-saving apology. For Anselm, creation radiates God's goodness. Sin compromises this objective goodness of creation. It dishonors God, but, even more, sin vitiates humanity, which stands before God guilty of subverting God's utterly beneficent design for all creatures. This guilty responsibility places humanity under moral obligation to make recompense to God. "So, then," Anselm states, "everyone who sins must repay to God the honor that he has taken away, and this is the satisfaction that every sinner ought to make to God."[3] This "ought" is not an obligation that might or might not arise in God's will, depending on God's capricious desire for an apology. It arises, rather, from the moral fact of sin and its corruption of God's objectively good plan for creation.

The moral obligation on the part of humanity to redress its sin, and the inability of humanity to do so, presents a bind from which the logic of sacrificial atonement emerges. While humanity is obliged to make satisfaction to God, humanity in its fallen state is unable to do so. Only a divine being is capable of restoring the divine honor, but, not being guilty of the offense, God is not obliged to do so. God could remit sin by mercy alone. But to do so, Anselm claims, would "not [be] fitting," for if sin "is neither paid for nor punished, it is subject to no law."[4] God's own faithfulness to the divinely willed order of justice leads Anselm to find a fitting logic in God's plan to save humanity by the Incarnation— the appearance in history of the God-human who has both the power to redeem and, at least through identification with fallen humanity in the Incarnation, the obligation to do so. "For God will not [make satisfaction]," Anselm concludes,

> because he does not owe it, and man will not do it, because he cannot. Therefore, for the God-Man to do this, the person who is to make this satisfaction must be both perfect God and perfect man, because none but true God can make it, and none but true man owes it.[5]

Anselm judges the Incarnation to be a living manifestation of God's loving, though just, response to sin, bearing in itself the harmony lost to creation by the human betrayal of God's will.

The mere appearance of the incarnate Son of God in history, however, does not cancel the debt that humanity owes to God for sin. Anselm insists that it is Jesus' suffering and death on the cross, willingly offered by Jesus to God as payment for humanity's sinful debt, that restores God's honor and rescues humanity from the death sentence that it justly deserves. In this act of sacrifice, the divine nature that could make payment, acting in union with the human nature that should make payment, sets right the disturbance wrought by sin. In some caricatures of Anselm's explanation, the sacrifice of Jesus on the cross is portrayed as a blood offering that a cold and distant father requires of an utterly blameless son, a terrible price paid for the appeasement of a divine honor that, as absolute and changeless, could never have been diminished in the first place by any creaturely act. Although it may be the case that some features of Anselm's account encourage this misrepresentation, it is important to remember that the doctrine of the Trinity is the backdrop for Anselm's reflections on sacrificial atonement. It is the one divine nature shared by both God the Father and God the Son that wills to make sacrifice for human sin. As terrible an event as Jesus' crucifixion is, it is an act that fulfills God's single, loving intention, accomplished at so great a cost, to raise humanity from the sinful consequence of death to the glory of eternal life.

For our purposes, it is crucial to note that the logic of Jesus' sacrificial exchange with sinful humanity presupposes his own innocence. If Jesus shared the sin of fallen humanity, he would stand under the same judgment of death that God righteously metes out to sinners. Within the assumptions of Chalcedon, of course, it would be completely inconceivable that the divine nature could be joined to share a human nature that existentially had perpetrated sinful rebellion against God. The logic of exchange requires that the sacrificial victim offered for the guilty represent them while yet being free of their guilt. Jesus' innocence assures the acceptability of his sacrifice and so its power. It is an innocence consistently shared by Jesus' divine and human natures, though it is typically divine and untypically human. For Anselm, Jesus' human innocence is unique after the Fall and, on the human side of the Incarnation, constitutes the condition for the reconciliation with God that he achieves for humanity.

Clearly, Anselm's theory of atonement proceeds from the assumptions of the legal explanation. Indeed, Anselm's theory is the tradition's most developed and influential account of how God's just retribution toward humanity is canceled by God's redeeming love. Its logic requires Jesus' innocence as a fitting condition of his sacrifice precisely because humanity is completely guilty without remainder. Moreover, it requires the uniqueness of Jesus' innocence. If Jesus' innocence were not unique, then a number of possible consequences would prevail, all of them unacceptable to the legal model of salvation. If Jesus' innocence were not unique, then his saving power would not extend completely to all, since some, at least in their innocence, would not be in need of his saving actions. The sacrificial logic of the legal explanation presupposes the total juxtaposition of innocence and guilt, the former placed utterly in the life of the savior and the latter in the sinful mass of fallen humanity. If Jesus' innocence were not unique, then his power to be the savior at all would evaporate. The logic of sacrifice dictates that purity becomes an offering for defilement. Jesus willingly exchanges his uncompromised innocence for humanity's uncompromised guilt, taking onto himself an undeserved death that is humanity's just lot. If Jesus' innocence were not unique but instead had counterparts in humanity at large, then, under legal assumptions, God's own innocence would become questionable. The admission of humanity's shared innocence with Jesus, even to a degree, would raise the specter of humanity's innocent suffering, and the prospect of God's guilt for allowing such suffering to occur at all.

The uniqueness of Jesus' innocence in Anselm's theory becomes a powerful justification for the tradition's denial of the innocent suffering of humanity. His account recognizes only one instance of humanity's innocent suffering in the share of humanity united to Jesus' divine nature in the Incarnation. Jesus' suffering becomes paradigmatic in this explanation, a source of consolation to some and a source of concern to others who find exemplary suffering to be an insidious justification for the humble submission often expected and commended to those who suffer violent abuse.[6] It is interesting to observe, though, that Jesus' *innocent* suffering is not paradigmatic, since its uniqueness presupposes and redresses humanity's utter guiltiness before God. In this respect, the innocence of Jesus' suffering distances it from the very suffering that it heals and with which it otherwise identifies.

We have seen that the emotional difficulties created by the denial of innocent suffering lead popular belief to supplement the legal explanation with the providential explanation's comforting assurances of God's good purposes amidst retributive death. Since Anselm's theory of atonement powerfully communicates the legal explanation, it should not be surprising that an equally powerful version of the providential explanation is woven into his theology.

One of the greatest challenges Anselm faces in his work involves offering a credible account of how Jesus' sacrifice on the cross could be both necessary and free. On the one hand, Anselm insists that Christ's atoning sacrifice is the solely reasonable way in which God could have saved the world, and, as exclusively logical, the atoning sacrifice is a necessity in the order of saving events. God could not have saved the world in another way, not because God is beholden to an imposed course of providence but because the necessity of sacrificial atonement is fixed by the confluence of God's love and justice in restoring fallen creation. This necessity, nothing other than the unchangeableness of God's providence in action, is what a faith-filled reasoning recognizes as the exclusive logic of sacrificial atonement. On the other hand, Anselm is concerned that this necessity not compromise Jesus' free decision to embrace the cross, a decision that Anselm judges to be crucial to the integrity of Jesus' sacrifice on behalf of humanity. "Christ himself," Anselm avers, "freely underwent death, not by yielding up his life as an act of obedience, but on account of his obedience in maintaining justice, because he so steadfastly persevered in it that he brought death on himself."[7] Yet, even though Jesus freely chose to sacrifice himself for the sins of the world, the "fitting" necessity of Jesus' sacrifice unavoidably leads to the difficult question of whether God willed the death of his Son for the world's redemption. Since Anselm has argued ardently on behalf of the logical necessity of Jesus' sacrifice, there is no way for him to avoid the conclusion that God willed the cross for Jesus.

That God wills Jesus' death may sound a dissonant chord in Christian sensibilities. Yet Anselm offers this judgment as a claim about God's love for humanity, even in the guilty depths of its fallenness. The Father wills the death of his Son for the sake of the world's salvation. In Anselm's trinitarian perspective, the one, divine nature shared by Father and Son wills the sacrifice of the cross so that humanity can be rescued from the death it deserves. The Son of God must pay a tremendous price in suffering to win humanity's eternal life. But this price is a measure of the Father and Son's shared love for humanity. Were salvation won in any other way, at least on Anselm's assumptions, it would compromise God's honor, the integrity of the divinely created order, and the very particular way in which that order was violated by sin. This single act of the divine will, shared by the Father and Son and freely accepted by the Son in the humility of the Incarnation, is the paradigmatic act of divine providence. Yet, in Anselm's explanation, it is an act of providence that is conveyed in a death willed by God. In light of Anselm's influence on the tradition, we can see his account of God's salvational dispensation in Jesus' death as a powerful justification for the popular belief in what I have called the providential explanation. As Christian sensibilities seek God's hand in their encounters with suffering and death, they need only turn to Anselm's sacrificial motif for an authoritative precedent. God can be providentially involved in every death because God was providentially involved in Jesus' death, willing it to occur for the grandest ends imaginable. Just as sacrificial logic concludes that God wills Jesus' death, and does so in a loving way, the believer can imagine that God wills the death of each and every person, not only as punishment but also as an expression of divine love.[8]

The idea that God wills death at all can be extraordinarily troubling to the life of faith, as we have considered earlier. That Jesus' death is representative in sacrificial logic may encourage believers to find a homology between Jesus' death and their own on the side of God's providential agency in death. But this same representativeness draws lines of sharp distinction between Jesus' death and the death of everyone else that undercuts any simple identification with Jesus' death, even within the assumptions of sacrificial logic. Jesus' death is not retributive punishment, while the death of everyone else is. Jesus' death brings about the world's redemption, while the death of everyone else does not. Jesus' death is the undeserved death of an innocent sufferer, while the death of everyone else is deserved and thoroughly guilty. Actually, we have seen that the popularity of the providential explanation stems from the desire to confirm, through God's actions, the very innocent suffering that the legal explanation denies. Unfortunately, in the judgment of so many believers, this indirect recognition of innocent suffering comes at the extraordinarily high price of God's arranging the particular circumstances of suffering and death that individuals find so grief-laden and tumultuous in their lives. My efforts to construct an understanding of God that denies both the legal and providential explanations requires a Christology that departs from the assumptions of sacrificial logic, particularly those that affirm God's agency in death and deny innocent suffering in any human life but Jesus'.

Solidarity in Innocent Suffering

The teaching of the Council of Chalcedon—that Jesus Christ is fully God and fully a human being—remains the measure of any orthodox description of the person and work of the savior. A Christology of innocent suffering is no exception to this rule of faith. Much recent theological inquiry has looked for new ways to conceive of the divinity of Jesus so that Chalcedon's talk about Jesus' shared "nature" with God will be more intelligible to the modern mind. Even though a meaningful conceptualization of Jesus' divinity may be a continuing theological challenge, belief in Jesus' full divinity is not a controversial issue in the Christian churches. As we have seen, it is Chalcedon's affirmation of Jesus' full and complete humanity that presents a problem for Christian belief. The difficult paradox of Chalcedon's "two-natures" doctrine, coupled with the infinite power Christians ascribe to Jesus' divine nature, makes it easy for Christians to embrace a mono-physitic understanding of the savior that diminishes Jesus' complete humanity in favor of even stronger emphases on his divinity. An adequate Christology, one that is faithful to the teaching of Chalcedon, will do as much justice to the claim that Jesus shares complete humanity with all human beings as it does to the claim that Jesus shares full divinity with God the Father. A Christology of innocent suffering will need to attend especially to this more controversial and, history has shown, more difficult belief.

The Council of Chalcedon does not simply teach that Jesus is one in being with us in humanity. It adds to that claim the doctrinal coda that Jesus is "like us in every respect except for sin." On the one hand, this coda is a qualification. It makes the point that Jesus is not a perpetrator of evil, as all other human beings are. In the language of my proposal, the coda insists that Jesus does not contribute to the history of precedent sin. On the other hand, it is important to see this coda as a statement of the fullest possible extent to which divinity embraces humanity in the Incarnation. If Jesus is like us in *every* respect except for sin, then Jesus shares all that is not sinful in humanity. So understood, the coda begins conceptually with all in human nature that is sinless and imagines the divine nature uniting itself to it in the mystery of the Incarnation. We could, however, understand this logic of identification by beginning on the side of Jesus' humanity and understanding human nature in general through Jesus' particular appropriation of it. If Jesus is like us in *every* respect except for sin, then humanity in principle must possess every dimension of Jesus' human nature. There are, of course, dimensions of human nature that are sinfully distorted, and Jesus does not have a share in such human fallenness. But according to the Chalcedonian coda, humanity lacks no human quality that Jesus possesses. On the face of it, this simple converse in Chalcedon's logic of identification says nothing different from the original premise. To traditional expectations, however, the converse makes a surprising claim about humanity. If humanity is like Jesus in every respect except for sin, then, one could argue, humanity too possesses the quality of innocence that is an existential condition for Jesus' innocent suffering. And more, if Jesus' innocent suffering is not sinful (and it could not be since Jesus endured it), then we have theological reason to posit innocent suffering as a dimension of human nature.

Such an interpretation of the rule of faith seems utterly unfounded when measured against traditional sensibilities. Understood along traditional lines, the Chalcedonian coda ascribes to Jesus a human nature purified of the sin of fallen humanity. But since humanity is thoroughly fallen here and now, in its real circumstances, the sinlessness of humanity that Jesus embraces fully could only be conceived of as the sinlessness of humanity before sin ever appeared in the world. And since, in that prelapsarian state of innocence, suffering had not yet entered the world as God's retribution for sin, no identification between Jesus' innocent suffering and the innocent suffering of humanity is possible. The traditional theology of retribution, represented so well in Anselm's sacrificial theory of atonement, makes humanity's utter lack of innocence after the Fall a function of the complete pervasiveness of human guilt and guilty suffering. Were we to depart from the logic of sacrifice and its theology of retribution, the Chalcedonian identification of everything sinless in humanity with Jesus' humanity validates the recognition of innocent suffering that besets humanity. Jesus' innocent suffering offers a paradigm for a sinless and yet suffering dimension of human experience that enables the innocent suffering of humanity to emerge from its eclipse in the theology of retribution.

If the innocent suffering of humanity can be justified by my reading of the Chalcedonian rule of faith, then we must seek a consistent theological explanation of how such innocent suffering is saved by God. Clearly, Anselm's sacrificial theory is not up to the task. The classical theology of atonement makes redemption a legal exchange in which Jesus offers to the Father his utter purity, conceived of as his innocent suffering, for humanity's utter defilement, conceived of as guilty suffering marked by the universality of retributive death. Recognizing innocent suffering in human lives, as my proposal does, undercuts Anselm's sacrificial logic. Affirming the innocent suffering of humanity compromises the uniqueness of Jesus' humanity and so its worthiness as an offering to God. Moreover, the logic of sacrifice assumes that human guiltiness in need of redemption is utterly complete, to the exclusion of innocence. Within this thorough guiltiness, suffering is punishment and innocent suffering is inconceivable, as is an account of how such an imaginary human condition might be saved by God. My affirmation of innocent suffering encourages us to think of Jesus' saving work not as sacrifice but as solidarity in the Incarnation with the innocent suffering of humanity, a point we can appreciate further by returning to the motif of promise.

Anselm's sacrificial theology places the cross at the center of God's saving action. A Christology that proceeds from the assumptions of promise rather than from the assumptions of sacrifice makes much of Jesus' resurrection from the dead as the fulfillment of God's biblical testimony to destroy death forever. In the event of Jesus' resurrection, God promises to do to all what God did to Jesus, namely, not to leave him (and all) in death but to raise him (and all) from death to eternal life. Jesus' resurrection is at once the promise made in its most specific and eventful way, and the completion of that promise in Jesus' new life. As believers await the fulfillment of God's biblical promise in their own lives, they rely on the history of the promise kept in Jesus as evidence for their own faith in resurrected life. Jesus' extraordinary precedence in this history lies not only in his resurrection as God's enactment of the promise of eternal life but also in the way Jesus meets the world's evil in his life, passion, and death. As an innocent sufferer rescued from death by God, Jesus, in the fullness of his humanity, stands powerless before death in exactly the way that all humanity does. Even in the fullness of his divinity, Jesus stands before death as in need of God's evil-defeating grace as all other human beings.

This is not to say that Jesus' innocent suffering is exactly like the innocent suffering of humanity at large. Jesus' innocent suffering is uncompromised by any sin or guilt on his part, while the innocent suffering so common in human lives always appears ambiguously in the company of guilt and sin. Jesus' innocent suffering is caused by precedent sin in which he plays no role as perpetrator, while humanity's innocent suffering is caused by a history of precedent sin to which the innocent victim contributes in other respects as victimizer. But in both cases, innocent suffering, whenever and wherever it appears, has a real integrity that is shared by both the Son of God and by humanity, and toward which God is disposed in his salvational deeds.

The innocent suffering that all human beings know in their lives is a particularly egregious manifestation of the power of evil. Innocent suffering tragically impresses us with the extent of its assault on the sensibilities of justice, dignity, and virtue. Innocent suffering is the most obvious and shocking symptom of evil at work in the world. Its presence in the created order, to say nothing of its prevalence, is a scandal to all who believe in the essential goodness of humanity and the abiding providential presence of God to all creation. In Jesus' innocent suffering, God identifies with humanity at the heart of evil's most powerful and scandalous presence to the human condition. God enters into solidarity with the innocent suffering that all human beings endure, and by doing so joins the community of moral witness that judges innocent suffering to be a terrible diminishment of life as it was originally created. God's omnipresence to all of creation is already and always such a witness, and we have seen that it is God's omnipresent witness in the life of the Spirit that testifies to the innocent suffering wrought by encounters with evil beyond the power of the human will, in the so-called "natural" occurrence of suffering and death. But God's presence to innocent suffering in Jesus' life becomes truly dramatic in the concreteness of Jesus' humanity, in the force of every one of his words and deeds, which decry suffering in all its forms, particularly the suffering of the innocent.

God's presence to innocent suffering becomes more dramatic still in the powerlessness with which Jesus faces and finally is overcome by death. This powerlessness of Jesus becomes God's most powerful witness to innocent suffering, for Jesus' own helplessness before suffering and death manifests God's compassionate closeness to the evil circumstances in which human suffering unfolds.[9] Jesus' innocent suffering becomes for believers an extraordinary medium of God's hopeful promise of eternal life in the midst of the suffering circumstances, much of it innocent, that the promise pledges to heal. As the Word made flesh (John 1:14), Jesus is the embodiment of God's promise to destroy death forever. In Jesus' embodied solidarity with humanity in its helplessness, he testifies on behalf of God to the meaninglessness of so much of the suffering that human beings bear innocently before the powers of evil at work in history. In this respect, Jesus' solidarity with innocent suffering exposes the viciousness with which both precedent sin and precedent evil bring their ruinous effects, whether willful or not, into human lives. Jesus does not assume the sinful debt of humanity in his suffering as he does in the sacrificial understanding of atonement. Jesus only assumes the final powerlessness of humanity before evil whenever it suffers innocently. His suffering in and of itself is not redemptive. Rather, his suffering manifests God's indictment of death and the many forms of deathliness constructed in the entire history of precedent sin. Whereas Jesus' miracles actively enact in small ways God's promise to defeat death, his suffering passively identifies the injustice of much human suffering at the hands of evil.

One can appreciate the full meaning of Jesus' resurrection from the dead as God's enacted faithfulness to the biblical promise in the light of Jesus' solidarity with those who suffer innocently. Although God's promise has not been fully kept for those who believe and hope in its fulfillment or for all of creation that, in Paul's words, longs to be saved (Romans 8:19) or for all of history whose future suffering has even yet to transpire, God's presence to innocent suffering in Jesus' passion and death attests to God's ongoing, compassionate solidarity with the very suffering that God has promised to heal fully. Jesus suffers powerlessly in his innocence before the world's violence, and in that suffering he shares in the powerless suffering of all humanity. Since he is the divine Son of God and sinless in his humanity, Jesus bears no responsibility for the evil that crushes his life. His innocent suffering, however, does not merit his resurrection from the dead. Innocent suffering is not an action he performs but instead a terrible injustice he endures. God's resurrection of Jesus demonstrates God's power to vanquish the very death before which all human beings eventually stand powerless. Jesus' resurrection is not his own deed but God's, and one through which God exhibits

in a most explicit way the future victory God will win for all eschatologically, when God's ongoing battle with evil is finally done.

The christological logic of promise brings us to a very different conclusion about God's disposition toward death from the
logic of sacrifice. If Jesus' resurrection is viewed as the fulfillment
of God's promise to destroy death gratuitously, then there is no
reason in principle to place death—Jesus' death or anyone's for
that matter—within the divine will. The scriptural words of
promise place death at odds with the divine will by promising its
destruction. If death is a reality (or better, a lack of reality) that
God intends to vitiate, any suggestion of death's inclusion in the
scheme of providence would contradict the very purport of the
promise by maintaining that God vows to destroy what God wills.
At first glance, this position may seem to place a limit on God's
power by its claim that God in no way wills the death of any person, in spite of the prevalence of death in the creaturely world.
Such a concern wrongly assumes that every act of the divine will
becomes enacted in time instantly and completely. As the very
logic of the divine promise attests to the foreignness of any death
to God's will, the event of Jesus' resurrection actually reveals that
death places no limit at all on God's power. Indeed, the only limit
on the divine power is a powerlessness God wills for God's own
being by embracing human helplessness before death in the event
of the Incarnation.

In a Christology of sacrificial atonement, Jesus' death is a saving death. Can the same be said for Jesus' death in the Christology of solidarity I have sketched here? My answer is both no and
yes. Jesus' death is not saving in the sense that the suffering of
Jesus' passion and cross cancel out God's just retribution for the
universality of human guilt. Jesus' suffering does not make anything right with God, as it does in Anselm's sacrificial theory.
Human beings, including Jesus, may find meaning in their lives,
in spite of the suffering that they inevitably endure. Suffering too
may be lived through and negotiated in any number of ways that
make suffering meaningful in the judgment of those who endure
it or witness to it. But suffering and death, in and of themselves,
are not charged with divine meaning. They are not means by
which God saves the world, nor are they conveyors of divine prov-

idence in any way. God has no hand at all in suffering and death, even in the suffering and death that overwhelmed the Son of God. Jesus' suffering is best conceived of as God's solidarity with humanity in the midst of its own innocent suffering. Jesus' suffering reveals God's judgment on death's dehumanizing power. When humanity is responsible for death, this judgment extends to humanity. When death is nonvolitional, God judges it no less harshly.

Jesus' death might be understood as a saving event to the degree that it becomes a manifestation of God's power over death in his resurrection of Jesus, which at once reveals and enacts God's promise to save all from death and suffering, so much of it innocent. God's resurrection of Jesus from the dead shows in the most explicit way how God continues to do battle with death in every human life and throughout all of history, and how God will finally win the battle for all just as God has won the battle for Jesus. Jesus' death is God's extraordinary closeness to the tragedy of guilty suffering and to the scandal of innocent suffering, both of which are ambiguously mixed in nearly every life. In order for this saving revelation and enactment to occur, God, in the divine nature of Jesus, did have to embrace suffering and death fully. And as the nonviolent sinlessness of Jesus' life exposed the empty power of precedent sin, there was a dull predictability in the fact that his death took place as a brutal capital punishment conducted with all the authority of the state in the name of law and order.[10] Even this terrible death could be understood as a saving event if placed within this loving dispensation of God toward death that culminates in Jesus' resurrection. But finally it is God's acting in Jesus to reconcile the world to Godself that is saving and not Jesus' suffering and death. Jesus' suffering and death, as the world's sinful violence toward Jesus' innocence, is as banal as any act of evil. There is nothing of God's providence in it.

An Ethics of Innocence

Christians have always believed in practicing Jesus' life. This is an amazing belief for Christians to hold in light of their belief in who

Jesus is. Jesus, Christians believe, is the unique Son of God. He is the incarnation of God's eternal, divine nature. To imitate the life of such a being would appear to be an impossible task in principle, since one dimension of his existence is so extraordinarily different, and divinely so, from the mere humanity of those who seek to imitate him. Jesus, of course, cannot be imitated in his divinity, if the success of imitation entailed the believer's becoming divine. No human being's action could ever be divine or bring human nature to the stature of divinity. Ancient Christians, especially in the traditions of the Christian East, did speak of the fullness of resurrected life as the divinization of the human person. But this intense description of God's powerful self-sharing in eternity never suggested that human beings are anything but creatures of God whose identity never becomes God. Moreover, Jesus cannot be imitated in his unique status as savior. He and he alone is the one through whom God makes the full meaning of his scriptural promise to destroy death forever. He and he alone is the resurrected one through whom God's promise of eternal life is accomplished and continues to be accomplished for all.

Following the Chalcedonian formula, Christians believe that Jesus is truly God as well as truly human. The Christian belief that Jesus is fully human is the basis for the expectation that Jesus' life is an ethical standard for believers that they are obliged to perform in their own lives. But even here, it would seem, the differences between Jesus and all of humanity obstruct the possibility of meaningful imitation. Jesus, after all, as the Chalcedonian coda teaches, is "like us in every respect except for sin." Humanity stands in a history of precedent sin that is unavoidable and inescapable, and that seduces all into sinful participation in evil. The claim that believers make about Jesus' sinlessness would seem to make him so different from all humanity that any meaningful imitation of his life would be impossible. The workings of imitation do require a measure of likeness between model and imitated practice that enables imitation to be seriously accomplishable. The same workings of imitation, however, require that the model imitated possess some measure of transcendence or otherness, that the model be more than the practice to a sufficient degree so that it is worthy of imitation and a guide to the lack or deficiency in the imitator. In these respects, Jesus' sinlessness is a meaning-ful condition of Christian discipleship and not a hindrance to it. Jesus shares humanity with all other human beings. By virtue of this likeness, believers may imitate his life. Jesus' sinlessness is not a dimension of his character that believers may achieve in their own lives. But this quality of Jesus' life, secured through his com-plete absence of guilt, may be imitated partially by believers in vir-tuous instances of innocence amidst their far more pervasive guilt.

We can understand Jesus' sinlessness as his acting innocently in every moral circumstance that he faced. Even though Jesus was fully human and lived a life in the midst of a history replete with evil, he never violated the bond of fidelity to God that he pos-sessed in his divinity for all eternity. Nor did he betray the human nature entrusted to him in the Incarnation by vitiating its creation in the image and likeness of God (Genesis 1:26; Philippians 2:5–11). Rather, Jesus remained faithful to both his divine and human natures by ever holding onto the innocent stature that is a product of his sinlessness. It would be easy for us to conceive of Jesus' innocence only as a passive trait, especially since his inno-cence is at once most striking and poignant in the suffering of his passion and death. Jesus' innocent suffering certainly possessed a kind of passivity, as all suffering does by its very nature. Yet, even in the powerlessness of his last hours, Jesus acted innocently. In his courage and compassion in facing his innocent death, and especially in his ready willingness to forgive his persecutors, Jesus showed the folly of retribution that accounts for so much of the world's suffering and death. In the course of his life, in every one of his words and deeds, Jesus put his sinless innocence into action to resist the evil that he encountered in his social world—in the malice of his contemporaries, in the many ways the social history of precedent sin has marginalized the poor and the afflicted among his fellow human beings, and in the pain and grief of sick-ness and death. If Jesus' life is any measure—and for believers it is the ethical measure sine qua non—then acting innocently can never finally be judged to be the stance of the silent observer or the passive bystander. All four Gospels portray Jesus' entire life as an innocent enactment of God's saving love for the world. But this innocence is one that aggressively opposed evil in all of its forms and that, even in the powerlessness of Jesus' death, revealed the fulfillment of God's promise to destroy evil forever through Jesus' resurrection from the dead.

This redescription of Jesus' innocence does not depart from the traditional assumption that Jesus *is* innocent, even if the implications of Jesus' innocence as presented here point us in new theological directions. What is novel in this Christology lies in the various ways that Jesus' innocence becomes paradigmatic for believers who, under traditional doctrinal assumptions, could not be innocent at all. Jesus' innocence becomes shareable as believers perceive it in their lives. Believers must be capable of innocence in order to recognize Jesus' innocence as a model both worthy of and capable of imitation. We have seen that a Christology of solidarity appreciates how Jesus' innocent suffering becomes paradigmatic for the innocent suffering of believers. Now we must consider how believers can embrace the way Jesus acts innocently throughout his entire life as a paradigm for Christian discipleship.

At one level, the question of how believers become true disciples has an obvious answer. Christians enter further and further into the commitment of discipleship by imitating Jesus' sinless innocence. By acting innocently as Jesus does, believers bring his life into theirs, and in such a way that they practice the resistance to evil that he did, actively, both powerfully by the practice of virtuous resistance and powerlessly by the practice of innocent suffering. In this respect, believers follow an incarnational paradigm, making the real, historical concreteness of Jesus' sinless innocence their standard for enduring and confronting evil just as Jesus did. Saying that Christians are obliged to act innocently in imitation of Jesus is not to say, of course, that believers will accomplish the innocent resistance of evil in the same way Jesus did. One of the ways in which Jesus' resistance is paradigmatic is the way it reveals the consequences of speaking and living the truth in our fallen world. History has shown repeatedly that those who resist the world's violence become its prey. Few imitators of Jesus are able to shake themselves free of the world's guilty entanglements to such a degree that their own innocent resistance will follow Jesus all the way to their own version of his cross. Contemporary prophets of justice and peace like Martin Luther King, Jr., Anwar Sadat, and Yitzak Rabin are all good examples of this kind of courageous resistance judged intolerable by a sinful world, even though only King would have understood his ethical commitments as a discipleship to the life of Jesus. Yet discipleship that is meaningful at all embraces Jesus' innocent acting intentionally and ardently, refusing to let the continuing presence of sin and guilt in any life serve as a ready excuse for a thoroughly tragic understanding of discipleship.

The ambiguity stirred by this portrait of the Christian life is most troubling to a traditional anthropology, which places all innocence in Jesus' life and all guilt in the lives of believers. Whereas a traditional understanding of discipleship acknowledges the importance of Christian virtue, whether explained as the work of grace or as human works cooperating meagerly with grace, it cannot entertain the thought of virtuous deeds being the authentic imitation of Jesus' innocence. This disjunction between the innocence of Jesus and the guilt of believers is the basis for the atoning exchange in the logic of sacrifice. But the logic of promise can also appreciate the real, though ambiguous, innocence of believers who are nevertheless guilty perpetrators of sin. The biblical promise enacted in Jesus' resurrection does not require that Jesus' innocence be played off against the complete guilt of humanity for salvation to be realized. The logic of promise only requires that God keep God's saving word. That innocence coexists with guilt in the fallen world has no bearing either on humanity's deep need for grace or on how God deigns to save the world. The workings of discipleship take place in a human community in which innocence and guilt are strangely mixed together, in which, we might say, the communion of the saints is just as much a communion of sinners[11] and the communion of the guilty includes in its same guilty members the communion of the innocent.

Believers have an obligation to imitate the innocent sinlessness of Jesus' humanity, and by doing so to resist the history of precedent sin that all humanity continues to perpetrate. The sinless innocence of Jesus' humanity reveals humanity's true nature

as God created it, before the history of precedent sin began, so to
speak. Believers, however, also have an obligation to imitate the
innocence of Jesus' divine nature. This seems like an odd thing to
say. Imitation, we have seen, requires a certain measure of shared
likeness in order to be meaningfully accomplished. Since Jesus'
divine nature is uncreated and human beings are but creatures,
imitating Jesus' divinity would seem to be beyond the capacity
and so the obligation of any believer. Believers could not imitate
Jesus' divinity in order to become divine. The infinite qualitative
difference in being between God and creatures, however, still
allows for a sharing in certain qualities that humanity and God
possess by virtue of the way God has graciously endowed the created order. The doctrine of humanity's creation in the image and
likeness of God means that all human beings in their own way possess divine qualities of being such as goodness, truth, and beauty,
as well as divine qualities of action such as love, mercy, justice,
and, of particular importance for our purposes, innocence.

The Christian tradition has always been willing to ascribe
innocence to human nature before the Fall or, in Catholic teaching, to an interim state after baptism and before the existential
guiltiness of responsible decision. Such innocence is always imagined as a passive virtue, as the absence of sin and guilt. My theological proposal encourages us to think of innocence not only as
a quality of being that human beings share with God in an ana-
logical way but also as an active virtue that believers enact in
order to imitate the divine nature of Jesus, the same nature that
Jesus shares with God who is Father and God who is Spirit. Believers, in other words, are called upon to do nothing less than imitate God's own innocent resistance of evil, to follow God in taking
up the struggle against evil in which God is engaged until death
is destroyed forever. In such an understanding, Jesus' shocking
words in the Sermon on the Mount—"Be perfect, therefore, as
your heavenly Father is perfect" (Matthew 5:48)—need not be
explained away as they have been throughout most of the Christian tradition. In opposition to the Catholic teaching that these
words articulate an optional ethics performed only by the most
extraordinary saints and the Lutheran teaching that these words
articulated an unaccomplishable ideal meant by repeated failure

to instruct the believer in human helplessness, an ethic of active innocence can understand the high expectations of these words as a call to all to imitate God's graceful action in doing battle with evil. The biblical promise enunciates God's commitment to bring this task to eschatological completion. The perfect accomplishment of this task is finally in God's power alone.[12]

The complicity of all humanity in the history of precedent sin and humanity's powerlessness over much of the power of precedent evil mean that believers will never perfectly realize Jesus' call to imitate God's innocent struggle against evil. This is not a minor failure. It is not a matter of falling short of the highest moral standard. Indeed, as history continues to show, the failure is often catastrophic, and so much so that many find little cause to hope that there is redemption of any kind before the horrendous suffering that human beings continue to commit. In the midst of this human tragedy, believers make a commitment in faith to God's infinite capacity to press the battle with evil where all human effort falls short, even in terrible ways. Given the prevalent power of evil in the world, particularly in human sinfulness, believers will often fail to achieve that active kind of innocence that I have described in these last pages. Though obliged to imitate Jesus in both his human and divine natures, believers often find that the insidiousness of evil brings their innocence, when they possess it at all, to the innocent witness of compassion for those who suffer innocently or to the innocence of their own suffering before the world's evil, so much of it the work of their own hands. In these powerless postures, both compassionate witness to suffering and suffering itself can take the form of a certain measure of activity that even reaches the effective level of passive resistance. Often, however, as the sad testimony of history reveals, evil's crushing power can be so overwhelming and irresistible that the powerlessness of suffering is complete and passive, and in that state nothing less than an abomination to everything and everyone good.

Faith is a stance committed to the same struggle with evil, with death and deathliness, to which the living God has pledged commitment for all time. Whatever faith knows of this struggle, it should know that God remains innocent before the world's evil,

and does not do so at the expense of human innocence but in solidarity with it. This innocence, shared by God and by human
beings, in their virtue and in their suffering, is the proper com-
portment of good persons toward evil. Innocence, we might say,
is a divine and human partnership, a moral disposition that gives
eternal and temporal testimony to evil's ultimate powerlessness
before the divine innocence and humanity's share in it. This innocence, in whatever powerful or powerless form it may appear, is
the work of the same divine grace to which it gives witness. It is
the enacted refusal to do death or to bring deathliness of any kind
to created life. Innocent is the way God always is and innocently
is the way God always acts. The life of discipleship follows God,
and God's incarnated presence in Jesus, by taking up the innocent
struggle to destroy death forever, the very struggle through which
God's biblical promise to enact the world's redemption is kept.

Notes

1. In what follows, I continue to think along with Ronald F. Thiemann, *Revelation and Theology: The Gospel as Narrated Promise* (Notre
Dame, Ind.: University of Notre Dame Press, 1985). I also rely on lines
of argumentation already developed in John E. Thiel, "Resurrected Life
and God's Biblical Promise," *The Month* 255 (January 1994): 4–11.

2. Henricus Denzinger-Adolfus Schönmetzer, *Enchiridion Symbolorum Definitionem et Declarationem de Rebus Fidei et Morum*, 34th ed.
(Freiburg im Breisgau: Herder, 1967), 108, no. 301.

3. Anselm of Canterbury, *Why God Became Man*, in *A Scholastic Mis-
cellany: Anselm to Ockham*, ed. E. Fairweather (Philadelphia: Westminster
Press, 1956), 119.

4. Ibid., 120.

5. Ibid., 152.

6. For an articulation of the criticism, made by many others, see Elis-
abeth Schüssler Fiorenza, *Jesus: Miriam's Child, Sophia's Prophet. Critical
Issues in Feminist Christology* (New York: Continuum, 1995), 98–107.

7. Anselm of Canterbury, *Why God Became Man*, 113.

8. Adela Yarbro Collins notes the connection between the logic of
sacrifice and the coincidence of retributive and providential wills in
God: "There is, I believe, a common experience that explains the fasci-
nation with human sacrifice and the reason that its metaphors are so
powerful. Human beings are subject to sudden variations in their expe-

riences and fortunes. From these experiences they infer a transcendent power which is double; a power that heals and kills, that blesses and curses, that gives and takes away. Because the idea of the total arbitrariness of this alternation is too hard to bear, people posit a principle of equilibrium and balance, whose disturbance must be restored by compensatory acts" (Adela Yarbro Collins, "Finding Meaning in the Death of Jesus," *Journal of Religion* 78 [1998]: 195).

9. Cynthia Crysdale speaks eloquently of the coincidence of Jesus' solidarity and compassion with sufferers in any adequate account of the cross as God's resistance toward evil. See Cynthia S. W. Crysdale, *Embracing Travail: Retrieving the Cross Today* (New York: Continuum, 2001), 64–68.

10. Walter Wink develops a Christology of Jesus' nonviolent engagement of structural evil in Walter Wink, *Engaging the Powers: Discernment and Resistance in a World of Domination* (Minneapolis: Fortress Press, 1992), 175–93.

11. Bradford E. Hinze makes this point about the communion of the saints, calling attention to the way a traditional conception of the *communio sanctorum* often assumes an exclusionary relationship between virtue and sin, particularly, he argues, by placing the actions of the institutional church always on the side of virtue. See Bradford E. Hinze, "Ecclesial Repentance and the Demands of Dialogue," *Theological Studies* 61 (2000): 232–33.

12. There is, though, a real difference between battling courageously against precedent sin and precedent evil, on the one hand, and accepting graciously the inevitability of suffering and death in every life, on the other. The ethics of innocence proposed here should not be understood to advocate extraordinary means to prolong life in the face of its inescapable loss, either through the cosmetic efforts of a youth-oriented culture or through the needless prolongation of life whose quality has been lost.

$$\text{·: :·}$$

Epilogue

ADOLPHE GESCHÉ HAS OBSERVED that "the West has not had a theology of the evil of misfortune, the evil suffered by the innocent."[1] I have tried to explain why this is so and to offer a theology of innocent suffering. My study focuses on the doctrine of God, but its attention to so many other central doctrines makes it a systematic theology in brief, and one that is rather untraditional in its consistent attention to the evil of innocent suffering.

As much as any writing on God and evil explains, it can only end with more questions. There are many questions that the reader might put to this study as it comes to a close. Some might want to take issue with my reading of the premodern, modern, and postmodern stances on God and evil, questioning my judgment that each in its own way denies innocent suffering before God. Some might question whether a Christology of solidarity can adequately portray the saving power of the person and work of Jesus Christ. Some might question the wisdom of retrieving the ancient dramatic battle motif, which seems so mythological and out of sorts with a contemporary mind-set. Some might think I have called on eschatological hope to provide a meaning that finally must crumble in the face of history's horrors.

It seems to me, though, that the most pointed question to my argument concerns whether I have actually rejected the dualism I was willing to risk in conceiving of God's relation to evil. The questioner might put it this way: "So, in your explanation, God is

172

the creator of the universe, and death courses through this universe, entering human lives as suffering that human persons encounter as evil, and yet neither God nor human persons are responsible for much of this death, and in any case not for the existential fact of death. How could death be so divorced from personal causality in a world created by a personal God?" This is a good question. But what makes it a good question is the expression it gives to the assumptions of the traditional theology of retribution, which aligns all evil with personal responsibility. The traditional theology of retribution is meaningful and effective. What else could explain its endurance for millennia? Yet, if my argument is cogent, the theology of retribution is also a source of emotional conflict that faith struggles to resolve, often in very convoluted ways.

My proposal is willing to leave the issue of death's cause behind, not by proposing the diminishment of divine power, as would process theology, but instead by tolerating this kind of ignorance while affirming that God does not do death, and indeed always works against it. Finally, my proposal offers a novel explanation of God's relation to evil. It claims that this construction is superior to the legal and providential explanations since it denies a double will in God and responds to the truthful experience of innocent suffering. This proposal does require the believer to accept ignorance about the causal origins of death encountered as evil. But any account of God's relation to evil, including the official legal explanation and the popular providential explanation, will have to admit ignorance at some point. I have maintained that doing so in the manner I have proposed accords better with the believer's experience of a providential, merciful, and loving God, as well as with the believer's undeniable experience of innocent suffering.

So much of the work of theology amounts to "getting God right" in thought and language. The academic environment in which theology has flourished can lead theologians to ignore the emotional lives of believers. This means that all good theology is pastoral. It tries to articulate the reality of God in a way that allows believers to experience more pointedly the God who has entered their lives as the God who saves, and as the God who saves in the face of the suffering they actually encounter. The more clearly the power of God's abiding providence toward a world fraught with evil is articulated, particularly the evil of innocent suffering, the greater the consolation believers can find in the God of promise. I hope that thinking and feeling about God in the way I have proposed will help believers find comfort in the midst of their own innocent suffering and encourage their resolve to stand with God in resisting the evil they endure and the evil they do.

Note

1. Adolphe Gesché, "Le problème du mal, problème de société," in *Théologie de la liberation* (Louvain-la-Neuve: Annales Cardijn, 1985), 33. Quoted in Gustavo Gutiérrez, *On Job: God-Talk and the Suffering of the Innocent,* trans. M. J. O'Connell (Maryknoll, N.Y.: Orbis Books, 1987), xv.

Index